Contents

Sagartia elegans variety *nivea*, Isles of Scilly.

Foreword

Anemones and corals (the anthozoa) are among the most colourful animals living in the waters around Britain and Ireland. Anyone who has spent time pottering around in rock pools will be familiar with one or two anemones, such as the beadlet anemone and snakelocks anemone. What this book reveals, is the great diversity of species that inhabit our waters, some of which, such as the multi-coloured jewel anemones will be familiar to divers, whilst others, such as the pink sea fan, are more elusive.

The fact that there are corals living in British and Irish waters may come as a surprise to many people who are more familiar with the concept of tropical coral reefs. But our own temperate seas support over 70 species of anemone and coral, including twelve species of coral. Anemones and corals have adapted to the widest range of habitats from the brackish shallows of estuaries and the silty depths of sea lochs, to wrecks and offshore deepwater reefs, and some even use other living creatures for their base. Most temperate coral species are solitary, but recently discovered deepwater reef-building corals highlight just how much more there is to learn about this group of species. These amazingly beautiful and often highly intricate animals are increasingly under threat from activities such as trawling, dredging and pollution, and climate change may yet prove a further significant threat. British corals and anemones lack none of the colour and beauty of warm water species and are sadly just as vulnerable to damage and destruction.

In this beautifully illustrated book, Chris Wood guides us through this colourful world of tentacles and polyps with photographic examples from the length and breadth of Britain and Ireland. Each species is carefully described with notes on its habitat and behaviour. The book concludes with an overview of the threats that face these fascinating and often fragile animals and how important it is that we take action to protect them for the future. Diver or non-diver, this book will take you on a guided tour of the anthozoan delights that abound in our seas.

Samantha Fanshawe
Director of Conservation
Marine Conservation Society

MARINE CONSERVATION
SOCIETY

Acknowledgements

These days an identification guide is only as good as the photographs used to illustrate it and I would like to thank all of those who contributed their images to the book, especially those who responded when asked to go out on a mission to photograph particular species. Almost all of them are involved in Seasearch in one way or another, whether as tutors, recorders or contributors to our stock of marine life photos for use in Seasearch training and projects. Special thanks to the main contributors, Bernard Picton (BP), Sue Scott (SS), Sue Daly (SD) and Paul Naylor (PN) but also to Rohan Holt (RH), Christine Howson (CH), Erling Svensen (ES), Richard Manuel (RM), Sally Sharrock (SSh), Peter Tinsley (PT), Chris Emblow (CE), Christine Morrow (CM), Francis Bunker (FB), George Brown (GB), Jack Laws (JL), Mark Woombs (MW), Maura Mitchell (MM), Mike Camplin (MC), Paul Parsons (PP), Steve Trewellha (ST) and Vicki Billings (VB). I would also like to thank Sue Daly (SD) for her lovely drawings. The pictures they have contributed are all marked with their initials, the remaining pictures are my own.

Many people have contributed to the contents of the book through discussions, exchanges of emails and their observations as divers. I would particularly like to thank Bernard Picton of the Ulster Museum, and Richard Manuel, whose Linnaean Society Guide has provided me with a mass of useful information and whose early Anthozoan Guide for the (then) Underwater Conservation Society provided much of the stimulus for the present book. Liz Sides of the National Parks and Wildlife Service in Ireland provided information on conservation measures in Ireland. Bernard Picton (Ulster Museum), Keith Hiscock (Marine Biological Association), Rohan Holt (Countryside Council for Wales) and Sue Daly all read the text in draft and have made useful and constructive comments and contributions. Marc Dando's design work has brought the whole book to life.

Finally thanks are due to the Seasearch sponsors, the Heritage Lottery Fund, English Nature, Countryside Council for Wales, Scottish Natural Heritage, Environment and Heritage Service (Northern Ireland) and the Joint Nature Conservation Committee whose financial support has enabled the book to go ahead after conventional publishers proved unwilling to produce a specialist guide of this sort.

Introduction

The scope of the guide

The animals included in this guide fall into the following nine groups:

Soft corals – colonies of tiny polyps with a soft fleshy body
Sea fans – colonies of tiny polyps with a flexible horny skeleton
Sea pens – tall colonies of polyps living partly buried in soft sediment
Stoloniferans – colonies of polyps rising from a thin encrusting membrane
Tube anemones – individual polyps living in a tube, usually buried in soft sediment
Colonial anemones – colonies of polyps with an encrusting common base
Sea anemones – individual polyps, usually attached to a hard surface
Corallimorpharians – individual polyps with a club-like tip to the tentacles
Hard corals – colonies or individual polyps with a hard calcareous skeleton

All of the anemones and corals fall within the Phylum CNIDARIA (pronounced Ny-daria). The name comes from the Latin *cnidae* meaning nettle and all of the members of the phylum have stinging cells which are used both for the capture of prey and for protection. There are three groups of cnidarians, the ANTHOZOA which are the subject of this guide, the HYDROZOA or hydroids and the SCYPHOZOA or jellyfish.

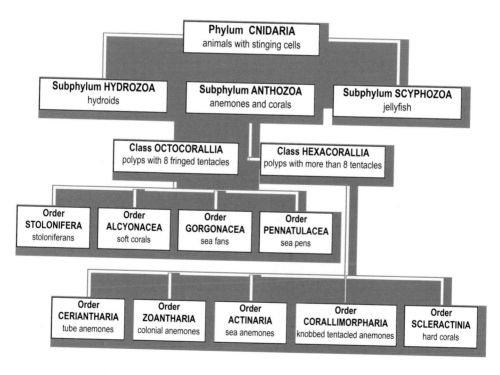

Structure of the anemone polyp

All of the **Anthozoa** are based on a similar structure, that of the **polyp**. This can be single, as in the case of most of the anemones and the cup corals, or it can be joined with other polyps in a colony, as are the soft corals, sea fans and many of the tropical hard corals.

The anemone or coral polyp has a hollow, cylindrical, body known as the **column**. The lower end may be joined by connecting soft tissues to other polyps in the form of a colony. It may have a basal disc which adheres to hard surfaces and allows some movement by muscular contractions. Alternatively it may be rounded and either burrow directly into soft sediments or live in a tube which itself is buried in sand or mud.

The column may be smooth or may have a series of suckers or **verrucae** either all over it, or just at the upper end. The upper end of the column has a collar in some species, especially the plumose anemone which is shown below.

The upper end of the column flattens into an **oral disk** which has a slit-like mouth at its centre and is surrounded by a number of **tentacles**. The tentacles are hollow and either simple, as in the hexacorals or with opposing rows of small offshoots, or **pinnae**, as in the colonial octocorals. The upper end of the column is known as the **parapet** and there may be a small valley between it and the tentacles known as the **fosse**.

From the mouth a flattened tube, the **actinopharynx**, leads internally into the body cavity or **coelenteron**. The internal surface of the actinopharynx has one or more longitudinal grooves with tiny hairs, or **cilia**, which can direct a current of water into the body. This is used both for respiration and to inflate or deflate the polyp by changing the hydrostatic pressure. The effect of this is most clearly shown in the plumose anemone which can change from being an erect anemone up to 20cm tall to an unattractive deflated blob, by decreasing the internal hydrostatic pressure.

The coelentron is divided up into a series of chambers by radially arranged walls of tissues known as **mesenteries**. These can often be seen as longitudinal lines on the column or as radial lines on the disc. The spaces between the mesenteries are known as **radii** and each one has a single hollow tentacle at its upper end. This means that the cavity inside each tentacle is linked directly with the body cavity. The mesenteries contain the reproductive, and digestive processes as well as muscular tissue.

Most of these features are shown below in the photograph and sketch of a small plumose anemone.

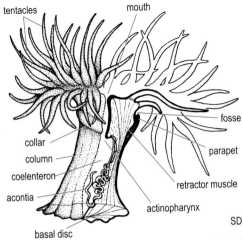

The arrangement of tentacles is one of the features that can be used to distinguish between species. Many species have concentric rings of tentacles with either six or ten in the innermost ring. These primary tentacles are usually the largest and may be held more upright than the remainder. The second ring normally has the same number of tentacles but following rings normally double in number of the last ring but decrease in size.

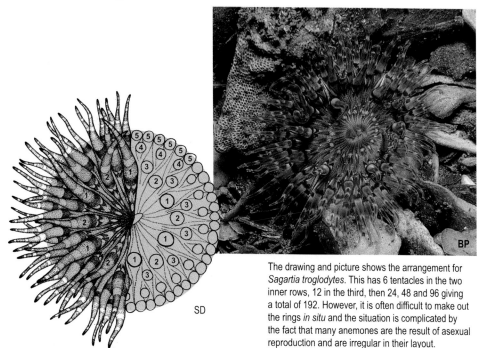

The drawing and picture shows the arrangement for *Sagartia troglodytes*. This has 6 tentacles in the two inner rows, 12 in the third, then 24, 48 and 96 giving a total of 192. However, it is often difficult to make out the rings *in situ* and the situation is complicated by the fact that many anemones are the result of asexual reproduction and are irregular in their layout.

Many anemones are able to contract the tentacles and oral disk into the body cavity for protection and when they are not feeding. The soft corals and sea fans are examples of colonial polyps which are able to contract into the common tissue mass or **coenenchyme**. Other colonial anemones are joined by a much narrower stolon which encrusts rocky and organic surfaces and does not provide any physical strength to the colony. Tube anemones can retract into their tube and many others, notably the plumose anemone, commonly retract their mouth and tentacles when there is little passing current. Other anemones are unable to retract their tentacles, the most common examples being the snakelocks and sea loch anemones.

Cnidae and feeding

All of the Cnidaria, including all sea anemones and corals, possess stinging cells, or **cnidae**, which are used both for defence and feeding. Each **cnida** is a microscopic, hollow, capsule which contains an inverted hollow tube which can be ejected with significant force and often pierce the tissues of prey or potential predators. Many of the cnidae possess toxins which can stun prey or sting predators. These toxins are best known to us in many species of jellyfish where the level of toxin is high enough to be felt by humans. We can also see cnidae in action by touching the tentacles of a snakelocks or beadlet anemone and feeling the way the tentacles stick to our fingers as the cnidae are discharged.

Cnidae come in two main categories, **spirocysts** and **nematocysts**. They are found in many of the tissues but tend to be concentrated in the tentacles, where they are of most value both in offence and defence. Some species possess nematocysts on long threads known as **acontia**. These are attached internally and can be used to subdue active prey which has been ingested. However the free ends can be extended out of the mouth and also used to deter predators. The species in which this is most often seen are the two anemones that live with hermit crabs, the parasitic and cloak anemones. In the photograph below the left anemone is using its acontia, possibly to deter a second hermit crab, also with an anemone attached.

Above: drawing of a nematocyst, un-discharged on the left and discharged on the right.   SD

Right: hermit crab with anemone emitting acontia. Loch Carron, Highland.

Whilst the food of most anemones consists of small organisms, a number of the larger species can be seen taking much larger prey. Dahlia anemones in particular are voracious feeders. The picture below (bottom left) shows an anemone in the last stages of eating a starfish and on page 50 there is one in the process of digesting a jellyfish. Anemones do not have it all their own way, however, as they in turn can be predated upon by starfish, nudibranchs and other mobile feeders. Soft corals appear to be particularly vulnerable. In the picture below (bottom right) a red cushion star, *Porania pulvillus*, is in the process of feeding on a dead men's finger.

Both photographs from Loch Carron, Highland.

Reproduction

Sea anemones and corals reproduce both sexually and asexually and some are able to do both. In sexual reproduction fertilisation may take place either internally or externally. Internal fertilisation can involve a period of brooding and the subsequent release of fully formed young anemones. This is known as **viviparity** and is most commonly observed in beadlet and daisy anemones. The photograph shows a daisy anemone in the process of ejecting fully formed live young from its mouth.

Loch Carron, Highland. SS

New colonial anemones and corals develop from a single larva which, after a short free-swimming period, settles on a suitable surface and develops into a singe ancestral polyp. Once established the single polyp can reproduce asexually, normally by budding (see below) and thus gradually build up a new colony.

Asexual reproduction takes place in all of the groups of sea anemones and corals except for the tube anemones (*Ceriantharia*). It occurs in four main ways:

Budding takes place in all of the colonial forms. In the case of the soft corals, sea fans, colonial anemones and colonial corals new polyps bud from the connecting tissue between existing polyps or even from the walls of existing polyps.

Longitudinal fission takes place in jewel anemones and some of the *Actinaria* (sea anemones) and in a modified form some of the hard corals. Here an existing anemone stretches itself by elongating its base and then splits in two across the middle, resulting in two new anemones of the same size. This process happens over a few hours. The picture shows a dahlia anemone in the process of splitting, having reached the stage where there are separate mouths but not all of the two rings of tentacles have been produced.

This method of reproduction is the reason that jewel anemones often occur in patches, each with a different colour. Jewel anemones, like many others, have a variety of colour forms but those forming a patch of one colour are likely to be all produced from one original anemone by a series of longitudinal fission processes.

Loch Carron, Highland. SS

Transverse fission is much less common and occurs where an anemone splits lengthways. In the case of two species, the trumpet and starlet, the anemone develops a constriction on the lower part of the column, which is eventually pinched off. The upper part grows a new base, whilst the lower part remains attached and generates a new disk, mouth and tentacles. *Gonactinia prolifera* grows a new ring of tentacles around the column before the anemones separate. This can be seen occurring in the picture of this anemone on page 48. Finally the wedge coral, which is free living, develops new disk, tentacles and mouth at the basal end and then separates in the middle.

Lands End, Cornwall.

Basal laceration occurs where small fragments of tissue separate from the lower part of the column just above the base. These then develop into tiny anemones. One common anemone that does this is the elegant anemone and is the reason why different colour varieties commonly cluster together. Another is the plumose anemone where there are commonly a number of small anemones clustered around the base of an adult which have all split off from it. This can be seen in the photograph.

The method of reproduction is one of the complicating factors in anemone identification. Those species which commonly reproduce by longitudinal fission or basal laceration often end up being irregular and losing the characteristic numbers and arrangement of rings of tentacles. One of the obvious signs of irregularity is the mouth which becomes three or more sided rather than a simple slit, as in the picture below.

Hand Deeps, Devon.

Species descriptions

In the descriptions of individual species that follow I have generally followed the taxonomic classification as set out in the MCS/Ulster Museum Species Directory. All of the species listed there as occurring in Britain and Ireland are referred to, though some rare or deep water species do not have full descriptions. However in the largest group, the *Actinaria*, which includes most of the sea anemones, there are so many species that they are grouped by habitat and behaviour so that species which could potentially be confused are close together. Where a species name is indented in the table which follows it is a rare or doubtful species which is referred to in the text but not fully described or photographed.

Summary table

The table gives summary information for each species. Where symbols are in bold type they are the main area, habitat or depth where the species occurs:

Distribution: the map shows the six areas used. There may be isolated records outsde the areas listed. Information for distributions has been taken from records in the Marine Nature Conservation Review (mermaid), the Biomar surveys and Seasearch observations.

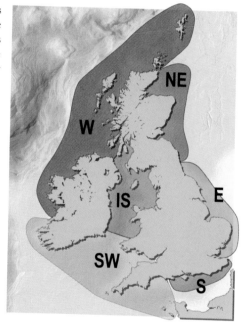

Habitat: this shows the habitats in which each species can be found. **Rock** includes reefs, boulders and stones, **Sand** includes coarse sand and gravel, **Living** denotes that the species is usually found on specific other animals or living on shells, both alive and dead. More information is usually given in the text.

Depth: **Shore** includes both the lower shore and rock pools and shallow sublittoral habitats down to about 10m depth, **Mid** depth is from 10m to 30m depth and **Deep** is below 30m.

How common: **Common** is widespread and regularly encountered, **Occasional** species have a limited distribution (within which they may be common), or are widespread but infrequently seen, **Scarce** is defined by the Joint Nature Conservation Committee based on records from the UK only, **Rare** is also as defined by the JNCC but also includes species so rare that they are not on the JNCC list or which do not occur at all in the UK but are found in Ireland or the Channel Islands. In these cases the Rare is in italics.

Size: is a guide to the maximum size across the disk and tentacles. **Large** is above 12cm, **Medium** 7–12cm, **Small** 2–7cm and **Tiny** less than 2cm.

Conservation status: those species covered by Biodiversity Action Plans or protected by the Wildlife and Countryside Act (UK only).

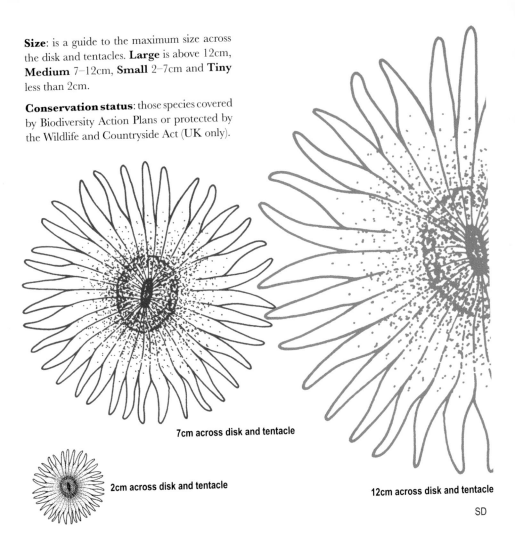

7cm across disk and tentacle

2cm across disk and tentacle

12cm across disk and tentacle

SD

Common Names

The great majority of anemones were given English names by Gosse (1860). Many of them have survived, such as plumose anemone and daisy anemone, even though the generic name has changed. Others have slightly changed. What we now call the snakelocks anemone was originally snake-locked. Other names have never really come into common use, such as glaucus pimplet and warted corklet. Some of the original names have been omitted intentionally as they are misleading. For instance Gosse called *Sagartia troglodytes* the cave-dwelling anemone as its specific name suggests. However we now know that these anemones are usually found in open sand and gravelly areas and not in caves so do not use the name. A few names are recent, such as elegant anemone for *Sagartia elegans*. Originally the colour varieties of this anemone were thought to be different species so Gosse does not have a name for the united species we now recognise. Most of Gosse's names end with the -let suffix denoting small.

SPECIFIC NAME	COMMON NAME	DISTRIBUTION	HABITAT	DEPTH	HOW COMMON	SIZE	CONSERVATION STATUS	PAGE	NOTES
Octocorallia Acyonacea	Soft corals							19	
Alcyonium digitatum	dead men's fingers	All	Rock	**Sh M D**	Common	Large		20	
Alcyonium glomeratum	red sea fingers	W IS **SW**	Rock	**M D**	Occasional	Large		22	
Alcyonium hibernicum	pink soft coral	W IS SW	Rock		Scarce	Small		23	caves and crevices
Octocorallia Gorgonacea	Sea fans							25	
Eunicella verrucosa	pink sea fan	**W SW S**	Rock	M D	Scarce	Large	BAP WCA	26	
Swiftia pallida	northern sea fan	W	Rock	M D	Occasional	Large		29	
Octocorallia Pennatulacea	Sea pens							31	
Funiculina quadrangularis	tall sea pen	W	Mud	**M D**	Occasional	Large		32	
Virgularia mirabilis	slender sea pen	W NE IS SW S	Mud	M D	Occasional	Large	BAP	33	
Pennatula phosphorea	phosphorescent sea pen	W NE	Mud	**M D**	Occasional	Large		34	
Octocorallia Stolonifera	Stoloniferans							35	
Sarcodictyon roseum		W IS SW S	Rock	Sh M D	Occasional	Tiny		35	
Clavularia sp.		W	Rock	M	Rare	Tiny		36	St Kilda only, undescribed
Cornularia cornucopiae		S	Rock	Sh	Rare	Tiny		36	Only one British record
Hexacorallia Ceriantharia	Tube anemones							37	
Cerianthus lloydii		All	Mud, Sand	Sh M D	Common	Medium		37	
Pachycerianthus multiplicatus	fireworks anemone	**W** SW	Mud	M	Scarce	Large		38	
Pachycerianthus indet.	'Dorothy'	SW	Rock, Sand	M	Rare	Large		39	Channel Islands only
Arachnanthus sarsi		W	Sand, Mud	M	Rare	Medium		40	

continued next page

SPECIFIC NAME	COMMON NAME	DISTRIBUTION	HABITAT	DEPTH	HOW COMMON	SIZE	CONSERVATION STATUS	PAGE	NOTES
Hexacorallia Zoantharia	Colonial anemones							41	
Epizoanthus couchii	sandy creeplet	W IS SW S	Rock	M	Occasional	Tiny		42	
Epizoanthus incrustatus			Sand	M D	Rare	Tiny		42	No recent records
Parazoanthus axinellae	yellow cluster anemone	W IS SW	Rock	M D	Scarce	Small		43	
Parazoanthus anguicomus	white cluster anemone	W SW	Rock	M D	Scarce	Small		45	
Isozoanthus sulcatus	ginger tiny or peppercorn	W IS SW S	Rock	Sh M	Occasional	Tiny		46	
Hexacorallia Actinaria								47	
Anemones that usually occur in groups or aggregations and related species									
Protanthea simplex	sea loch anemone	W	Rock, Living	M D	Common	Small		47	
Gonactinia prolifera		W SW	Living		Rare	Tiny		48	
Urticina felina	dahlia anemone	All	Rock, Sand	Sh M D	Common	Large		49	
Urticina eques	horseman anemone	W NE All	Rock, Sand	M D	Common	Large		51	
Stomphia coccinea	swimming anemone	W NE	Rock, Living	M D	Occasional	Medium		53	
Bolocera tuediae	deeplet sea anemone	W NE	Rock	M D	Occasional	Large		54	
Aiptasia mutabilis	trumpet anemone	SW S	Rock, Living	Sh M D	Scarce	Small		55	
Metridium senile	plumose anemone	All	Rock	Sh M D	Common	Large		56	
Sagartia elegans	elegant anemone	All	Rock	Sh M	Common	Small		58	
Actinothoe sphyrodeta	sandaled or fried egg anemone	W IS SW S	Rock	M	Common	Small		61	
Anemones that live on the shore or in shallow water									
Actinia equina	beadlet anemone	All	Rock	Sh	Common	Small		65	
Actinia fragacea	strawberry anemone	SW S	Rock	Sh	Occasional	Small		66	
Actinia prasina		IS	Rock	Sh	Rare	Small		67	

Species	Common name	Distribution	Habitat	Zone	Frequency	Size	Status	Page	Notes
Anemonia viridis	snakelocks anemone	W IS SW S	Rock, Living	Sh M	Common	Large		68	
Aulactinia verrucosa	gem anemone	W IS **SW**	Rock	Sh	Common	Small		70	
Anthopleura ballii		SW S	Rock, Sand	Sh	Occasional	Small		71	
Anthopleura thallia	glaucus pimplet	W **SW**	Rock, Sand	Sh	Scarce	Small		73	
Diadumene cincta		E All	Rock, Living	**Sh** M	Occasional	Small		74	
Aiptasiogeton pellucidus		SW	Rock	Sh M	Rare	Tiny		75	
Haliplanella lineata	orange striped anemone	W SW S	Rock, Living	Sh	Rare	Small		76	
Phellia gausapata	warted corklet	W NE SW	Rock	Sh	Occasional	Small		77	
worm anemones									
Edwardsiella carnea		**W SW** NE	Rock	Sh M	Occasional	Tiny		78	
Edwardsia claparedii		W IS SW S E	Mud, sand	Sh	Occasional	Small		78	
Edwardsia delapiae		SW	Sand	Sh	*Rare*	Small		78	Valentia Is. only
Edwardsia timida		**W IS**	Sand	Sh	Scarce	Small		78	
Scolanthus callimorphus		SW W	Sand	Sh	Rare	Medium		78	
Nematostella vectensis	starlet anemone	S E	Mud	Sh	Scarce	Tiny	BAP WCA	80	
Edwardsia ivelli	Ivell's anemone	S	Mud	Sh	Rare	Tiny	BAP WCA	80	Shoreham only
Anemones that live on soft sea-beds									
Aureliania heterocera	imperial anemone	W IS SW	Rock, Sand	M	Occasional	Medium		81	
Anemonactis mazeli		IS SW S	Sand, Mud	**M D**	Scarce	Small		83	
Sagartia troglodytes		All	Sand, Mud	Sh M	Common	Small		84	
Sagartia ornata		?	Rock, Living	?	?	Tiny		85	
Cereus pedunculatus	daisy anemone	All	Sand, Mud	Sh M D	Common	Large		86	
Sagartiogeton undatus		W IS SW S	Sand, Mud	Sh M D	Occasional	Small		87	
Sagartiogeton laceratus		all	Sand, Mud, Living	M	Occasional	Tiny		88	
Halcampoides elongatus	night anemone	W IS SW	Sand, Mud	M	Rare	Small		89	
Halcampoides? abyssorum		W SW	Sand	M D?	*Rare*	Large		89	

continued next page

SPECIFIC NAME	COMMON NAME	DISTRIBUTION	HABITAT	DEPTH	HOW COMMON	SIZE	CONSERVATION STATUS	PAGE	NOTES
Mesacmaea mitchellii	policeman anemone	W IS SW	Sand	M	Scarce	Medium		90	
Peachia cylindrica		All	Sand	Sh M D	Occasional	Medium		91	
Halcampa chrysanthellum		All	Sand, Mud	Sh M	Occasional	Tiny		92	
Hormathiidae Anemones that live on other animals									
Calliactis parasitica	parasitic anemone	W IS SW	Living	Sh M	Common	Medium		93	
Adamsia carcinopados	cloak anemone	All except E	Living	Sh M	Common	Small		95	
Amphianthus dohrnii	sea fan anemone	SW	Living	M	Rare	Tiny	BAP	97	
Hormathia coronata		W IS SW	Rock, Sand, Living	M D	Occasional	Small		99	
Cataphellia brodricii	latticed corklet	SW W	Rock, Sand	Sh	Scarce	Small		100	
Hormathia digitata		(NE E)	Living	M D	Rare	Medium		101	
Hormatia alba		W	?	D	Rare	?		101	
Paraphellia expansa		W IS SW	Sand	?	Rare	?		101	
Actinauge richardi		(W)	Sand, Mud	D	?	?		101	
Hexacorallia Corallimorpharia	Corallimorpharians							103	
Corynactis viridis	jewel anemone	W IS SW S	Rare	M	Common	Small		103	
Hexacorallia Scleractinia	Hard corals							105	
Caryophyllia smithii	devonshire cup-coral	All except E	Rare	M D	Common	Small		106	
Caryophyllia inornata	southern cup-coral	W IS SW S	Rare	M D	Rare	Tiny		108	
Balanophyllia regia	scarlet and gold cup-coral	SW	Rare	Sh	Scarce	Tiny		109	
Leptopsammia pruvoti	sunset cup-coral	SW	Rare	M	Rare	Small	BAP	110	
Sphenotrochus andrewianus	wedge coral	All	Sand	M D	Rare	Tiny		112	
Holpangia durotrix	Weymouth carpet coral	SW	Rare	Sh M	Rare	Small		112	
Lophelia pertusa	deep water coral	W	reef building	D	?	Large	BAP	113	

Soft Corals
Octocorallia, Family Alcyoniidae

Soft corals are colonial animals that form either encrusting sheets or erect fleshy masses, often with finger-like branches. The surface is covered in large numbers of individual polyps. The polyp has eight tentacles, each of which has two rows of tiny offshoots along it. These are known as pinnate tentacles. The body is strengthened by the presence of tiny calcareous splinters within it called sclerites.

Soft corals are usually attached to rocky surfaces though they may occur on other stable surfaces such as cobbles and large shells.

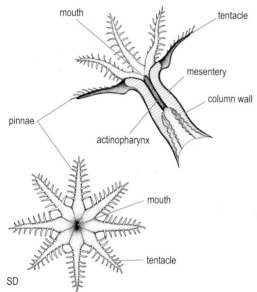

Photo and drawings of polyps of the red sea finger *Alcyonium glomeratum*.

Soft corals reproduce by asexual budding. New polyps bud from tubular connections between existing polyps or directly from the walls of the polyps themselves.

Soft corals have a worldwide distribution and are found at all depths from the lower shore to at least 9000m. However, there are only three species in British and Irish waters, one of which, the dead men's finger, is very common.

Dead men's fingers and red sea fingers can be found together in south-west England. Eddystone, Devon.

Alcyonium digitatum Dead men's fingers

Orange and white colour forms and extended and contracted polyps. St Abbs, Borders.

A wall covered in dead men's fingers. St Abbs, Borders.

This common colonial soft coral has an orange, yellow or white body with blunt, finger-like projections up to 25cm tall. The polyps are found all over the body. They are translucent white in colour and closely spaced giving a furry outline when they are extended to feed. When not feeding the smooth and rather bloated looking fingers show how the common name arose.

Dead men's fingers are common around all British and Irish coasts on rocks and boulders, and occasionally on cobble and shells, from the lower shore down to about 50m. They also occur throughout the North-east Atlantic as far south as Portugal. As filter feeders they prefer areas with some current and can withstand turbulent conditions. Places where they are particularly common are in the north-east around St Abbs and the Farne Islands, and current-swept channels in the entrance to sea lochs in western Scotland. Here you can often see them mixed with brittle stars.

Two creatures commonly live and feed on dead men's fingers. These are the large sea-slug *Tritonia hombergi*, particularly in Scottish waters, and the false cowrie, *Simnia patula*, most often seen in Devon and Cornwall.

The different colour forms are found together in many places and there does not seem to be any regional or habitat difference between them. White forms may be a little more common in the south and most colonies on the west coast of Ireland are orange.

New colonies arise from the dispersal of free-swimming larvae which can survive in the plankton for long periods. This ensures a wide dispersal of larvae and allows new colonies to form on new substrates and accounts for the wide UK distribution. The larvae settle and develop into an ancestral polyp which then creates a colony by asexual budding.

Dead men's fingers have a dormant period over the autumn and winter when the polyps are permanently retracted and the whole colony may become discoloured and covered in filamentous red algae and other material. The covering material will be expelled in the early spring when the colonies spawn and begin to feed again.

Dead men's fingers are long living and can survive for over 25 years.

Top right: dormant colony with algal cover. Isle of Man.

Right: *Simnia patula* adult (centre) and eggs (bottom). The Lizard, Cornwall.

Bottom: *Tritonia hombergi* eating dead men's finger. Loch Carron, Highland.

Alcyonium glomeratum Red sea fingers

Expanded and contracted colonies. Manacles, Cornwall (above) and Lundy, Devon (below).

Colonies can sometimes be pale yellow or even white. St Marys, Isles of Scilly.

This colonial soft coral has a deep red body with slim 'fingers' growing up to 20cm tall. The polyps are spread all over the body and are translucent white, contrasting with the red body colour. When the polyps are retracted the body has a warty texture and can look rather deflated.

Red sea fingers are found on steep or overhanging rock surfaces, usually out of but close to areas of strong water movement. They can be found from 10–50m but are more common below 20m. They are easily distinguished from the more common dead men's fingers by their red body colour and more spiky appearance caused by the thinner fingers and more widely spaced polyps.

Red sea fingers have a restricted distribution in the Britain and Ireland, occurring in the English Channel west of Portland, the Channel Islands (where they are more common than dead men's fingers), both coasts of Devon and Cornwall, the Isles of Scilly and a few sites in western Wales and western Scotland. They also occur on the west coast of Ireland.

Alcyonium hibernicum Pink soft coral or Pink sea fingers

SS

An extensive group of pink soft corals from southern Ireland.

This tiny soft coral grows either as small fingers up to 4cm tall or as a thin encrustation with the polyps on slightly raised nodules with a clear area between them. British specimens are mostly pink with a white rim below the tentacles of the polyps giving a slightly spangled appearance.

The taxonomy has been recently revised by McFadden (1999). In most books and references the name *Parerythropodium coralloides* has been used but this is now thought to be a more southerly species. *Alcyonium hibernicum* has been identified as a separate species based on specimens from the Isle of Man and Ireland and it is assumed that other British records are of this species.

This is a scarce species and not often recorded. In addition to the Isle of Man and Ireland there are records from the Channel Islands, Devon, Cornwall, south Wales and various sites on the west coast of Scotland and at St Kilda. It is particularly common in sea caves in the south of the Isle of Man.

The pink soft coral is nearly always found under overhangs or in caves, well out of the light and sheltered from water movements.

Partly contracted colony. Isle of Man.

A large, healthy pink sea fan, *Eunicella verrucosa*. Eddystone, Devon.

Sea fans
Octocorallia, Order Gorgonacea

The sea fans, like the soft corals, are octocorals and their polyps have eight fringed tentacles. The colonies are branching and each branch is a rod like structure which is calcified and strengthened with internal bone-like fragments known as **sclerites**. The colonies usually branch in one plane and are commonly aligned at right angles to the prevailing water current so that each polyp benefits equally from passing food. The colony as a whole is flexible enough to withstand water movement, though it does not tolerate strong turbulence, and is easily snapped off by physical contact.

Polyps occur all along the branches in an irregular fashion though they are mostly aligned along the plane of the colony as a whole. They can be retracted into the skeleton.

Sea fans are usually attached to rocks though they may attach to other stable surfaces such as wrecks and boulders.

Sea fan colonies grow by the process of asexual budding. New polyps bud from tubular connections between existing polyps or directly from the walls of the polyps themselves. New colonies are formed by the settlement of planulae larvae from the zooplankton. The larva grows into a single polyp but by the time the colony is 1cm tall it will have three or four. Studies of the pink sea fan in south Devon have shown that young colonies may grow by 6–7cm per year whilst established ones grow much more slowly, only about 1cm.

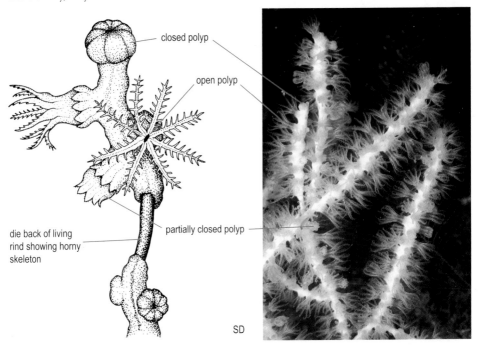

closed polyp

open polyp

partially closed polyp

die back of living
rind showing horny
skeleton

SD

Sea fans have a worldwide distribution and there are many species, some of which grow to 3m across. There are only two species in British and Irish waters though 20 have been recorded from the European Atlantic coasts and the Mediterranean. These include the precious coral, *Corallium rubrum*, the source of red coral jewellery.

Eunicella verrucosa Pink sea fan

Part of a sea fan 'forest'. The Manacles, Cornwall.

Small pink sea fan. The Manacles, Cornwall.

This sea fan has a distinctive, many branched, growth form and normally forms a distinctive fan shape with all of the branches in a single plane. The usual size of fully grown colonies is about 30cm tall and 40cm wide but recent diver surveys have recorded them up to 100cm across in the Channel Islands. Pink sea fans are commonly found on open rocky surfaces at depths of 20m or more where there is little turbulence but may occur shallower in some sheltered conditions such as inside the breakwater at Plymouth. Occasionally colonies are bushy rather than fan shaped. This is where local currents are either very weak or multi-directional.

In some areas very large numbers of pink sea fans grow close together in a 'forest' with up to 20 fans per square metre. This usually occurs on deeper flat bedrock or on the flattened plates of wrecks.

Despite its name the colour is variable from white to yellow to an orangey-pink. The pink form is the most common in British waters though occasional white or buff colonies occur. However the pink sea fan is usually white in southern Ireland and at some sites both colours occur. In southern Europe and the Mediterranean they are all white.

Since the sea fan is usually aligned across currents it can become fouled by drifting organisms such as seaweeds. Dogfish often use them to attach their egg cases, or mermaid's purses, to and some animals, such as barnacles and bryozoans, settle on them. There is even an anemone which lives exclusively on sea fans and other rod-like animals (see *Amphianthus dohrnii* on page 97).

There are few animals that actually prey on sea fans, most are repulsed by the stinging nematocysts in the tentacles. However the nudibranchs or sea slugs have adapted to feed on various anemones and corals as well as many other animals. The sea slug that is found on the sea fan is *Tritonia nilsodhneri*, which is well camouflaged to look like the sea fan itself. *Tritonia* lays its characteristic spirals of eggs around sea fan branches. The false cowrie, *Simnia patula*, (see page 21) has also been seen feeding on sea fans.

The pink sea fan is a southerly species in Britain and Ireland. It is common on channel coasts west of Portland and in the Channel Islands and all around the south-western peninsula, including the Isles of Scilly and Lundy. Smaller numbers occur as far north as Skomer and the St David's Peninsula in Wales and along the south coast of England east of Portland as far as Poole Bay. In Ireland it is found on western coasts as far north as Donegal. Outside the British Isles it also occurs throughout the north-east Atlantic, south to north Africa and in the Mediterranean.

Dogfish egg case wrapped around a pink sea fan. Salcombe, Devon.

A white colony fouled by fishing line, algae and debris. There is an unusually large number of nudibranchs living on the colony. Isles of Scilly.

Whilst the pink sea fan does not provide a suitable material for coral jewellery it has been collected in the past to be dried as a decoration, and much damage has been done by fishing gear. Since 1992 it has been a protected species in Great Britain under the Wildlife and Countryside Act (1981). This means it is an offence to kill, injure or take a sea fan or to be in possession of a live or dead animal or offer it for sale. Awareness of the species amongst fishermen is being increased to minimise damage from trawling, an initiative in Lyme Bay is one example. Whilst divers are unlikely to be prosecuted for breaking a sea fan it is one species they should be particularly careful of when underwater. A careless kick with a fin could kill a fan which might be up to 50 years old.

As a part of the UK's response to the International Biological Diversity Convention it is one of a very small number of marine species for which a Biodiversity Action Plan has been prepared.

Sea fan nudibranch eggs (left) and adult (below).
The Lizard, Cornwall.

Swiftia pallida Northern sea fan

A whole colony (above) and a close up of part (right).
Firth of Lorn, Argyll & Bute.

This sea fan has relatively few branches which are arranged in an irregular fashion. It is much more straggly in appearance than the pink sea fan. British specimens are white or pale grey in colour though red or pink forms of the same species occur in the Mediterranean. Colonies are up to 20cm tall.

The northern sea fan is found on flat and sloping rock surfaces and occasionally on boulders, usually below 20m.

In the British Isles this species is known only from the west of Scotland from around Oban northwards, the Inner and Outer Hebrides and the Kenmare River in south-west Ireland, the only place where both British and Irish species of sea fans occur. Elsewhere it has been reported further south, from the Bay of Biscay and the Mediterranean, where it occurs as deep as 600m.

Diver with *Funiculina quadrangularis*. Loch Sunart, Highland.

Sea Pens
Octocorallia, Order Pennatulacea

Sea pens, like the soft corals and sea fans, are octocorals and their polyps have eight fringed tentacles. They are unique in that they are the only group of octocorals that live exclusively on muddy or sandy sea-beds. Each colony has a central stalk, the lower part of which is free of polyps and functions as a burrowing organ. This is the part of the sea pen which is buried in the soft sediment. The upper part of the stalk is known as the rachis and bears the polyps either directly on the stalk itself or on pairs of branches.

Most sea pens are capable of luminescence during darkness. This can occur either as isolated flashes or rhythmic pulses of light passing along the whole colony.

There are three British species of sea pens, one of which is widespread. The most likely places they will be encountered by divers is in muddy bottoms of Scottish sea lochs.

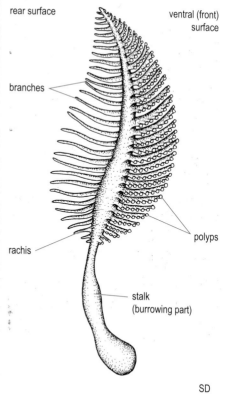

rear surface

ventral (front) surface

branches

polyps

rachis

stalk (burrowing part)

SD

All three species can occur together as here off Oban in 30m.

Funiculina quadrangularis Tall sea pen

This is the largest of the British and Irish sea pens and can be up to 2m in length. The polyps are distributed along the stalk and the colony is not branched. About a fifth of the colony is buried in the mud. The long colonies have a distinctive curved shape, rather reminiscent of the sea whips of tropical waters. The colour of the colony is white, yellowish or pale pink.

The stalk has a square cross section which has given the animal its specific name *quadrangularis*.

This sea pen has been recorded on western coasts of Britain and Ireland. It has a very wide distribution and may be found worldwide. Diver records all come from sea lochs along the west coast of Scotland, in depths of 30m or more. Here it is often found with the Norway Lobster or scampi. The deep water brittlestar *Asteronyx loveni* is known to cling to sea pens.

It has been suggested that this sea pen was formerly much more common and that populations have been severely reduced by the effects of scampi trawling. The dead remains can sometimes be seen dumped in fishing ports where nets and trawls are cleaned. Tall sea pens cannot retract into the sediment, though they can pull themselves upright again after gentle disturbance.

The colonies (which are of separate sexes) are believed to have a pattern of patchy recruitment, slow growth and have a long life span. This makes a population less able to recover from damage than other species.

Because of the threats *Funiculina* is one of the species for which a Biodiversity Action Plan has been prepared.

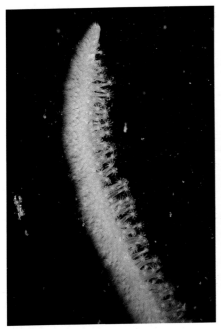

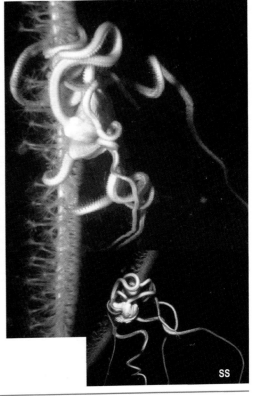

Above: the top of a *Funiculina* colony.
Oban, Argyll and Bute. See also page 30.

Left and inset: deep water brittlestar *Asteronyx loveni* on a sea pen.

SS

Virgularia mirabilis Slender sea pen

This sea pen is the one most likely to be encountered by divers in British and Irish waters. It is up to 60cm tall and about half of the total length is buried in the sand and mud in which it lives. It has a mucus lined burrow into which the whole colony can withdraw quite quickly if disturbed.

The central stalk is straight and round in cross section. The polyps are on paired branches and there is frequently a bare length of the central stalk at the top of the colony. The length of the side branches tapers towards the top and bottom of the colony producing a delicate profile. Colour is white to yellow and this species is able to luminesce in darkness.

Like the other sea pens, the slender sea pen is found on deep muddy bottoms but it can also be found in shallower sheltered waters, and thus frequently occurs in larger harbours where there are undisturbed sandy and muddy areas. In these situations it may be as shallow as 10m.

The slender sea pen is most commonly found on northern and western coasts of Britain and Ireland. In Scotland it has been recorded by divers most often between Mull and Shetland, in Ireland between Carlingford Lough and Rathin in the north and from a number of sheltered sites in the west. Southerly records are very limited but populations have been reported from locations such as Holyhead harbour, Portland harbour and Plymouth Sound.

Firth of Lorn, Argyll and Bute.

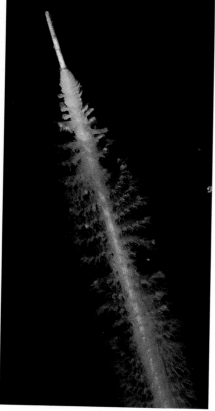

Loch Goil, Argyll and Bute.

Pennatula phosphorea Phosphorescent sea pen

This is the most stout and fleshy of the three British and Irish sea pens. It is up to 40cm long, of which up to 25cm is exposed above the surface. The branches are triangular in cross-section and arranged alternately on opposite sides of the central stalk, rather than in pairs. As its name suggests it is capable of blue/green luminescence when stimulated. Its main stalk is white but the branches and polyps are pale pink. This species has sclerites in the body that are deep red giving the colony not only its strength but also its reddish overall colour. It is a particularly beautiful animal, all the more so for being found in often dark and muddy conditions.

The phosphorescent sea pen is able to retract into the sediment in which it lives. It is also sometimes found bent over in a partly limp state when not actively feeding.

Like the other sea pens *Pennatula* is most commonly found in western Scottish sea lochs and normally on sheltered muddy bottoms below 10m. It has also been reported from Shetland and off the Northumberland and Durham coasts.

Front (left) and rear (right) views of *Pennatula*. Oban, Argyll and Bute.

Stoloniferans
Octocorallia, Order Stolonifera

The stolonifera, like the soft corals, are octocorals and their polyps have eight fringed tentacles. The individual polyps arise from a slender, more or less tubular stolon. There are three recorded British species all of which are small and easily overlooked. Only one of them is at all common. Stoloniferans can be easily confused with the sessile stage of jellyfish and this is dealt with at the end of this section.

Sarcodictyon roseum

This species forms an encrusting network of 2mm wide flattened stolons on rocks and shells, from which the polyps arise singly. Each polyp is up to 10mm tall, including its tentacles and is semi-translucent white in colour. The stolon is typically red but it may be white or colourless. It is often overgrown with other life and only the polyps are visible as in the photograph.

This species grows on rocks, stones and shells. It is occasionally found in shaded places on the lower shore but is more commonly encountered below low water mark and has been recorded as deep as 100m. It is found on all coasts of Britain and Ireland but is easily overlooked because of its small size.

Top: cluster of polyps adjacent to a carrot sponge. Southbourne, Dorset.

Right: polyps visible with the stolon completely covered by detritus. Mulroy Bay, Donegal.

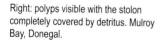

Undescribed stoloniferan probably *Clavularia* sp.

Another stoloniferan has been recorded on a number of occasions from St Kilda, Scotland, but not elsewhere. This forms clusters of polyps which are denser than those of *Sarcodictyon roseum*. The polyps rise from longish extensions to the stolon which are often covered in small particules, giving a rough surface. This is unlike *Sarcodictyion* where the polyps rise almost directly from the stolon.

The identity of this stoloniferan is uncertain as no specimens have been collected. It is most likely to be a species of *Clavularia*.

Two pictures of the undescribed stoloniferan from St Kilda, (right) with polyps extended and (left) with polyps contracted, showing the stolon.

The only other stoloniferan likely to be encountered is *Cornularia cornucopiae*. This is a southern species that is common in the Mediterranean and has only been recorded in British waters from the shore in Dorset. The polyps are up to 20mm tall and the stolon is much more slender than that of *Sarcodictyon*. This is a species that might well occur in the Channel Islands but there do not appear to be any records of it.

Aurelia aurita Moon jellyfish

The moon jellyfish has an unusual life cycle which includes a period when it is attached to rocky surfaces and closely resembles a stoloniferan. Following a brief swimming period new planulae larvae attach to hard surface and develop into tiny sessile animals known as scyphistomae. These reproduce by asexual budding and eventually release free-swimming tiny immature jellyfish. Whilst attached to the rock there are commonly huge numbers of the tiny scyphistomae giving white fluffy appearance. They are usually found in shallow water and underneath overhanging surfaces.

Moon jellyfish scyphistomae.

Tube anemones
Hexacorallia, Order Cerriantharia

The tube anemones are the only group of anemones to live in a felt or partchment-like tube buried in sand and mud. They all have two series of tentacles – short labial tentacles around the mouth and a larger number of longer marginal ones on the edge of the disk. The anemone can move within the tube, which has a smooth and slippery lining, enabling it to retract rapidly when disturbed. Unlike most anemones they cannot retract the tentacles into the soft column. Retracting the whole animal into the tube has the same effect. The tube is commonly much longer than the animal itself. The juveniles are planktonic and free swimming. Once settled the tube is constructed from many discharged nematocyst threads, and mucus-bound external material.

Cerianthus lloydii. Plymouth, Devon.

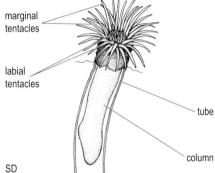

marginal tentacles

labial tentacles

tube

column

SD

Cerianthus lloydii

This is much the most common and widespread of the tube anemones. It has up to 70 marginal tentacles which may have a span of 70mm. The colour of the tentacles is often brown but they may also be green or white. Mixed colours often occur in same area and may give the impression of being different species.

This anemone is widespread all around all Britain and Ireland except in parts of the North Sea coast. It is found on sand, mud and gravel substrates and even amongst maerl. It occasionally occurs on the lower shore but is usually sublittoral, being found to depths of 100m or more.

Left: brown specimen in sand, Islay, Argyll and Bute. Right: greeny-white specimen in maerl, Kilkeiran Bay, Galway.

Pachycerianthus multiplicatus Fireworks anemone

PN

BP

This is a much larger anemone than the more common *Cerianthus lloydii*, and is a spectacular sight, particularly since it contrasts with the muddy sea-bed in which it lives. It has up to 200 marginal tentacles with a span of up to 300mm and lives in a tube which may be up to 1m long. The marginal tentacles are whitish with brown bands and are characteristically held with the base part upright and the ends flowing in whatever water movement there may be giving a very graceful appearance.

This anemone is only known in British waters from western Scottish sea lochs such as Loch Duich, Loch Sunart, Loch Fyne and Loch Goil. All are fijordic sea lochs with a shallow water sill at their entrances. It is usually found in very sheltered situations towards the head of the loch. It is also known from similarly sheltered areas in the west of Ireland.

Three differently coloured anemones one with white tentacles from Loch Duich, Highland (above); one with brown banded tentacles from Loch Goil, Argyll and Bute (top left) and a light coloured specimen from Kilmackilloge Harbour, Kerry (bottom left).

A partly closed anemone showing how the long tentacles curl when retracting. Loch Duich, Highland.

SS

Pachycerianthus indet. 'Dorothy'

SD

Jersey, Channel Islands.

This anemone is very similar to *Pachycerianthus multiplicatus* though it is not quite so large. It has up to 150 marginal tentacles with a span of up to 200mm. The tentacles are much less likely to be banded but there is a dark brown area at the base which seems to be a consistent feature. Unlike the fireworks anemone it is found in areas of rocks and gravel rather than mud.

The taxonomic status of this anemone is uncertain and it does not appear to have been formally described or named. The name Dorothy is an affectionate name coined by Richard Manuel for an individual specimen in an aquarium! There is a very similar species in the Mediterranean known as *Cerianthus membranaceus*.

The only part of the British Isles from which this species is known is the Channel Islands. It also occurs on the adjacent coast of Brittany.

However there is a single record of *Pachycerianthus multiplicatus* in the MNCR database (mermaid) from a rocky habitat in south Cornwall. In view of the location and habitat this is almost certainly this undescribed species and not *P. multiplicatus*.

Firth of Lorn, Argyll and Bute.

This anemone has the fewest tentacles of the British tube anemones, 30 inner labial ones and 30 long marginal ones. The inner labial tentacles are held together pointing upwards to form a cone which is characteristic of the species. The whole animal may protrude up to 200mm from the tube. It is found in sand or shelly mud at depths from 10–36m. It may be partly nocturnal, a feature of other anemones of this genus found in tropical waters.

This is a very rare anemone which has been only recorded from a few sites in western Scotland and north and north-west Ireland.

Top: Rathlin Island, Antrim.

Bottom: A small *Arachnanthus* which has only 20 tentacles. Additional tentacles will grow as it reaches full size. Firth of Lorn, Argyll and Bute.

Colonial anemones
Hexacorallia, Order Zoantharia

All of the British species of this group of anemones are colonial. They consist of a number of polyps growing from an encrusting conenchyme attached to rocks and stones. This part of the colony is often covered over with sand or bryozoan or hydroid 'turf'. The polyps of the different species are very similar. The disc is a little wider than the column which gives a delicately fluted appearance to the polyp when looked at in profile. There are two circles of tentacles which are found on the edge of the disc, one of which is usually held up and the other flat.

The colonies grow in size by budding off new polyps from the common base. This is known as extratentacular budding. New colonies are formed from the distribution and settlement of planula larva.

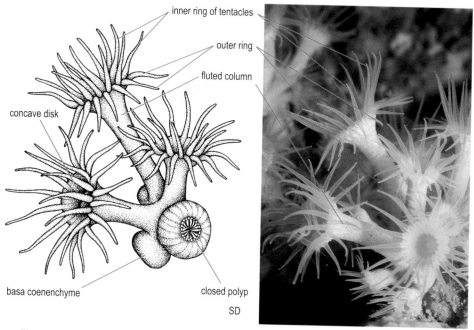

inner ring of tentacles

outer ring

fluted column

concave disk

basa coenenchyme

closed polyp

SD

There are four species of British and Irish zoantharians included in this book, all of which are quite small and easily overlooked. There are also a number of other species that have only been found in very deep waters offshore or for which there are no recent records.

Epizoanthus couchii Sandy creeplet

The polyps of this colonial anemone are small, up to 10mm tall and 5mm in diameter, and arise from a thin narrow base which is attached to rock or shells and is often covered in sand or other detritus. The tentacles are translucent white with a tiny white tip and the remainder of the body semi-translucent buff or pinkish. There are between 24 and 32 tentacles and the column has a serrated parapet.

Lighter coloured colonies can be confused with *Parazoanthus anguicomus* (page 45) but the polyps are smaller and the tentacles of *E. couchii* are longer than the width of the disk whilst those of *P. anguicomus* are similar or shorter.

The sandy creeplet is found on rocks and shells and sometimes forms extensive networks which seem to attract sandy particles, hence its common name. It is widespread in occurrence on south and west coasts of Britain, but is rare in Ireland and absent from the east coasts of England and Scotland. However it is easily overlooked because of its small size and tendency to retract the polyps.

Specimens from Lough Hyne, Cork, showing the long tentacles with white tips.

A typically buff coloured colony with silt covering the basal coenenchyme. Loch Long, Argyll and Bute.

Other similar species

Epizoanthus incrustans

There are two known forms of this anemone. One grows over gastropod shells and completely replaces the shell over time. There are up to 20 polyps in each colony each of which is up to 15mm tall and 6mm in diameter. The other form has little or no basal encrustation and the polyps either radiate from a central point or bud from the walls of others. The polyps are thought to be similar to the sandy creeplet. Both forms are inhabitants of sand and gravel and found in depths of 20–200m. This species has been recorded in the past from a number of different localities around British coasts but there are no recent records and no photographs of living specimens.

Parazoanthus axinellae Yellow cluster anemone

This colonial anemone forms dense clusters of polyps arising from a common base which is normally visible. Its colour is usually pale yellow with a contrasting area of much darker yellow or orange around the mouth. There are up to 34 slender and pointed tentacles on each polyp and the polyps are up to 15mm tall.

This anemone can be confused with *Epizoanthus couchii*. However the tentacles are shorter in relation to the body and the yellow cluster anemone does not retract so readily when disturbed, making it an attractive photographic subject.

Parazoanthus is found both on rocky and organic surfaces in depths from 6–100m. It is most commonly encountered by divers on rocky surfaces in 20–30 metres. It prefers shaded surfaces just out of strong currents and may be near the base of the rocks close to sand but just above the scour zone.

It is a generally southerly species in Britain and Ireland and also occurs around south-western Europe and in the Mediterranean. British records are from Devon, Cornwall, the Channel Islands and South Wales though it also occurs at Bardsey Island and the Llyn peninsula in North Wales, St Kilda and a number of sites on the north and western coasts of Ireland.

Isles of Scilly

Hilsea Point, Devon

An unusually white form of *Parazoanthus axinellae*. Jersey, Channel Islands.

Parazoanthus anguicomus White cluster anemone

A typical Scottish colony. Firth of Lorn, Argyll and Bute.

This is the largest of the colonial anemones with polyps up to 25mm tall and up to 44 tentacles which are not much longer than the width of the disk. The polyps are not very densely arranged and the colonies often form extensive sheets rather than discrete clumps. Colonies are usually found in dark locations such as overhangs, crevices, the roofs of caves or on wrecks. The colour is dull to bright white.

The white cluster anemone is similar to white coloured *P. axinellae* but can be distinguished by the larger size, more robust appearance and proportionally shorter tentacles.

Parazoanthus anguicomus is largely a northern species with most sightings being in west Scotland, the Hebrides, St Kilda and Shetland as well as parts of northern and western Ireland. There are records from further south however, including Lundy North Devon and on the south coasts of Devon and Cornwall. Many of the records in the south are from offshore locations or wrecks.

Right: a southerly colony on a wreck off Penzance, Cornwall.

PN

Isozoanthus sulcatus Ginger tiny or peppercorn anemone

SD

CH

This distinctive little anemone is dark brown in colour and commonly found in silty areas in considerable numbers. Its polyps are only 4mm tall and 2mm in diameter and have between 19 and 22 tentacles. The common base of the colony is usually covered in fine silt or other debris. The polyps often stand out against their silty surroundings but they are very shy and will retract if disturbed.

The anemone is found in open rock pools on the lower shore and in the shallow sublittoral on silted rock, stones and shells. It is commonly recorded around south and west coasts of England and Wales as far north as Anglesey and east to Sussex, from south-west Scotland and from many locations on the south and west coasts of Ireland. In the south it is found in the Channel Islands and down into north and west France.

Above: Jersey, Channel Islands.
Left: Mullaghmore, Donegal.

Sea anemones
Hexacorallia, Order Actinaria

Anemones that usually occur in groups or aggregations, and related species

Most of this group of anemones usually occur in closely spaced groups. They are not colonial animals but individual anemones which cluster together, usually as a result of their reproductive strategy. Also included here are some closely related anemones which have physical similarities but are not found in groups.

Protanthea simplex Sea loch anemone

Sea loch anemones on rock. Loch Carron, Highland.

This is a northerly species which was not thought to occur off British coasts until quite recently. However it is now known to be common in Scottish sea lochs.

The sea loch anemone is a delicate and attractive looking species with long slender tentacles which, unusually, cannot be retracted into the column. There are up to 200 tentacles with a spread of up to 70mm. They are translucent white with a somewhat frosted appearance. The column is smooth and flared at the top with a translucent white or light pink colour. ·

The anemone has an unusual 'collapse' behaviour in which it loses all muscular strength and hangs limply down from the attached disk. This is a temporary behaviour and presumably represents a resting phase that in other anemones would be accompanied by retracting the tentacles into the column. It is also often only loosely attached and can become detached from the rock and move through the water with jerky movements of its tentacles

It is a sociable anemone and in suitable locations there may be many individuals close together. In a Scandanavian survey a density of 2000 anemones per square metre was observed. It is found on open rock faces and other firm surfaces such as wrecks, sea squirts and worm tubes.

Almost all of the records from shallow waters come from sheltered locations in Scottish sea lochs. It has not been recorded in England, Wales or Ireland. However *Protanthea* is also known from much deeper water, up to 400m, around Rockall and in Scandinavia.

Top left: a sea loch anemone on a sea squirt.
Loch Linnhe, HIghland.

Bottom left: floating sea loch anemone in mid-water.
Loch Goil, Argyll and Bute.

Right: deflated sea loch anemone amongst normal individuals.
Loch Goil, Argyll and Bute.

Gonactinia prolifera

This is a tiny anemone which could be confused with small *Protanthea*. It is only 5mm tall, including the tentacles, and has about 16 non-retracting tentacles which are relatively large. The colour is a translucent white or pink. It is well known for its swimming ability though is normally found attached to seaweeds, worm tubes or sea squirts. It is rather a rare anemone with records from Plymouth, Northern Ireland and Scottish sea lochs and islands.

An anemone in the process of reproducing by transverse fission. A second column and set of tentacles has been produced prior to breaking away from the original anemone below.
Loch Carron, Highland.

Urticina felina Dahlia anemone

A group of dahlia anemones in a typical habitat where rocks run into gravel. Aran Islands, Galway.

A half closed anemone showing gravel fragments stuck onto the column. Anvil Point, Dorset.

The two species in the family *Urticina* are two of the largest of the British sea anemones. The dahlia anemone is up to 20cm across the tentacles, which are short and stout and arranged in multiples of ten. The column is covered in small grey warts, which usually have gravel or shell fragments attached to them as in the picture of a half closed anemone. The colour is very variable and the disc may be either plain or patterned with the tentacles banded or plain and often contrasting in colour from the disk. Different colour forms may occur together as in the picture from the Aran Islands. This anemone is one which is thought to only reproduce sexually, hence there is no clustering of individuals of a similar origin as in the case of anemones that reproduce by laceration or fission.

This anemone is found both on the lower shore and sublittorally down to at least 100m. It occurs on rocks, shells and stable gravel sea-beds and may form dense carpets in crevices, gullies and wave-exposed locations. In such situations it can represent a high proportion of the biomass. It is an active feeder on anything that comes within range of the stinging nematocysts. This can include prawns, young fish or even something as large as a jellyfish (see photograph).

The dahlia anemone is a slow growing and long lived species. Although there is little information from *in situ* observations, aquarium specimens have been known to live for over 50 years.

This is a very widely distributed anemone and may occur in cool temperate areas all around the northern hemisphere. In the US it is known as the northern anemone. It is common around all of the coasts of Britain and Ireland.

An anemone in the process of ingesting a jellyfish. St Abbs, Borders.

Colours are very varied but show a consistent pattern. St Brides Bay, Pembrokeshire.

Urticina eques Horseman anemone

A pink and buff specimen with a typically red-streaked column, Loch Nevis, Highland

This anemone is placed here in this guide because it is very similar in shape and variety of coloration to the dahlia anemone and the two species are easily confused. The horseman anemone grows larger, up to 35cm across the tentacles. Its tentacles are similarly stout, though they may be a little longer, and are also arranged in multiples of ten. The main difference is in the column which in the case of the horseman anemone does not have adhesive warts and consequently does not have gravel and other fragments attached to it. There are small pale spots on the column but these are not adhesive. Though there is a good deal of variety of colour the column, disk and tentacles often have shades of pink or red on them. A streaked form with patches of red and buff on the column, as in the picture above, is common.

Urticina eques is exclusively sublittoral but occurs in the same sorts of habitat as the dahlia anemone, often in gullies and at the base of rocks where they meet sand and gravely areas. The two species can often be seen together.

Uticina eques is less widespread than the dahlia anemone though it occurs on all coasts of Britain and Ireland, except for south-west England where it is very rare. It is often confused with the dahlia anemone, especially where the two species occur together, but the size, colour and lack of warts on the column are usually sufficient features to distinguish the two.

A closed specimen with a red column, smooth and without any gravel attached. Loch Long, Argyll and Bute.

Two pictures of the same, white, anemone expanded and closed. St Abbs, Borders.

Stomphia coccinea Swimming anemone

Left: a partly contracted anemone in a muddy area with particles on the column. Loch Etive, Highland. Right: a fully expanded specimen, St Abbs, Borders. In both cases note the broad base to the column, usually covered in detritus, which is wider than the span of the tentacles.

This anemone is included here because of its close similarity to the two preceding species though it does not occur in groups. Its common name comes from the ability of anemones of this group, in response to approaches by starfish, nudibranchs or other predators, to release their hold on the substratum and perform jerky movements with the extended column allowing them to move clear of danger. Other members of the family which occur elsewhere in the world, are better able to do this than this particular species which has only be observed to jump clear of the sea-bed momentarily.

The swimming anemone has a broad base, often wider than the disk and up to 60mm. The tentacles are relatively short and characteristically arranged. There are six tentacles in the first ring and these are often held upwards over the mouth (compare with *Mesacmea mitchellii*). The colour is very similar to *Urticina eques*, with reddish hues and often with two red bands on the tentacles.

The swimming anemone can be found on stones and shells, often on the large horse mussel, *Modiolus modiolus*. It is entirely sublittoral, occurring as deep as 400m.

Stomphia has a wide distribution, occurring throughout the circumpolar regions of the northern hemisphere. In Britain it is most common on North Sea coasts, though it has been recorded more widely, excluding the extreme south.

Loch Fyne, Argyll and Bute.

Bolocera tuediae Deeplet sea anemone

JL

Above: St Abbs, Borders. Below: Loch Nevis, Highland.

Bolocera is a large anemone which is rather similar in size and form to the two large *Urticina* species, which is why it is included here. However it has a different colour and is found in different situations. It has up to 200 long tentacles which are usually held in a regular and graceful fashion. They have a slight constriction around the base of each tentacle and are capable of shedding tentacles by pinching them off by muscular action. The reason for this is not known. It can grow to a large size, up to 30cm across the tentacles. The colour is usually white but it can be pink, buff or even orange. The tentacles are never banded and are the same colour as the column, which is also plain.

This anemone is always found sublittorally, usually deeper than 10m. It has a northerly distribution in the British Isles and is best known from north-east England and south-east Scotland. It also occurs in the outer parts of some west Scottish sea lochs. Gosse named it deeplet because the specimens he had were from deep water, though the diminutive –let is hardly appropriate for one of our larger anemones.

Aiptasia mutabilis Trumpet anemone

A group of anemones amongst algae and branching bryozoans. Brixham, Devon.

The trumpet anemone (originally trumplet) is named after the shape of its long smooth column, which has a trumpet shaped flute at the top. The tentacles, of which there are about 100, are long, stout at the base but taper to a fine point. Those closest to the mouth are longer than those on the edge of the disc. They do not usually retract though they are capable of doing so. The span of the tentacles is up to 15cm. The colour is a greeny brown, often streaked with white or blue from the mouth across the disc to the base of the tentacles.

The trumpet anemone is often found in large numbers where it occurs. It is one of the few anemones that is known to reproduce both asexually by transverse fission and also by viviparity. In transverse fission a constriction occurs on the lower part of the column, which is eventually pinched off. The lower part rapidly grows a new disc and tentacles whilst the separated upper part grows a new base, usually rather more slowly. Viviparity is a form of sexual reproduction in which the larvae are released as fully formed young anemones.

A single specimen in gravel. Lulworth Cove, Dorset.

The trumpet anemone is found on the lower shore and sublittorally down to 100m. Divers see it most often in shallow water where it is attached to rocks, in crevices amongst boulders and cobbles or even attached to kelp holdfasts. It is a southerly species in the British Isles being found along the south coast of England west of Selsey Bill, in the Channel Islands and around the south-west peninsular as far north as Lundy. There are records from South Pembrokeshire and Bardsey Island in Wales. Elsewhere it occurs around northwest France and most of south-western Europe as well as in the Mediterranean. The Mediterranean specimens are larger and have banded tentacles and there is some doubt as to whether they are genuinely the same species. The British variety, described and pictured here, was formerly called *Aiptasia couchii* and the two species were only combined in 1972. The trumpet anemone is nationally scarce, though where it does occur there may be large numbers.

Metridium senile Plumose anemone

Brown and white specimens, with small anemones around the base. Summer Isles, Highland.

The plumose anemone in its most common form is a large and conspicuous anemone which is unlikely to be mistaken for anything else. However there is also a smaller form which is less distinctive. Both forms have an adhesive base which is wider than the column. The column is long and smooth and there is a distinct collar or parapet near the top. The tentacles are numerous and slender.

The large 'plumose' form has been described by some authors as the variety *dianthus*. It is the largest sea anemone in British waters and may be up to 30cm tall and with a spread across the tentacles of 15cm. In older specimens the disc may be waved or folded forming lobes. The tentacles are short and there may be several thousand of them giving a characteristic fluffy appearance to the anemone. They are normally all one colour with little differentiation between the column and the disc, typical colours being white, orange and, less commonly, green. Some individuals have an orange column with white tentacles.

The small form is the variety *pallidus*, which does not exceed 25mm across. The disc is flatter, not waved as in the larger variety, and there are not normally more than 200 tentacles. The column is shorter, not usually any taller than it is wide. It is not clear whether the two forms are distinct varieties or variants resulting from different environmental conditions.

The plumose anemone is a very social animal and in favourable conditions there are often large numbers of individuals closely packed together. They often completely cover the sides of wrecks or harbour walls, if the water current is strong, and give them a completely white appearance. They are capable of movement by contraction and expansion of the base allowing them to slide along. This allows the colonisation of new areas. As an example if a mooring rope is tied to a wreck which has plumose anemones on it, they will soon begin to move up the rope to take advantage of the passing food in the current. One of the things that helps plumose anemones to become dominant species in suitable habitats is their ability to use 'catch tentacles' to sting adjacent fauna and discourage colonisation.

Both sea spiders and the large nudibranch *Aeolidia papillosa* have been reported to predate on plumose anemones.

Plumose anemones normally reproduce by basal laceration, though sexual reproduction also occurs. In basal laceration small pieces of flesh from the base of an adult anemone tear off and generate new animals around the base. It is common to see large individuals with a number of small ones around the base (see photograph). Because of this method of reproduction there are often large numbers of one colour form together.

Above: closely packed orange anemones. St Martins, Isles of Scilly.

Left: close up of a white specimen showing the parapet at the top of the column and the lobed oral disc. Isle of Man.

The large size of this anemone is partly because of its ability to pump itself up with water when feeding. When the current is slack the anemones often deflate and the tentacles are retracted inside the column, which is left with a small hole inside the contracted collar.

This is a very common anemone and is found on all coasts of Britain and Ireland. It occurs from the lower shore to 200m depth. Elsewhere in the world it occurs on both the Pacific and Atlantic coasts of North America. It has been introduced to the Adriatic Sea and South Africa. The small *pallidus* form is more common on the shore and in shallow waters, including brackish creeks and estuaries. The large *dianthus* form is exclusively sublittoral and prefers areas with strong water movement. They may be attached to rocks, piers, wrecks and pipes.

Above: a number of the small '*pallidus*' form of plumose anemones. Daugleddau Pembrokeshire.
Below: a group of anemones, some partly or wholly contracted. Lewis, Hebrides.

SS

Sagartia elegans Elegant anemone

This is a common anemone but one which is very variable in colour and consequently easily confused. The tentacles are relatively long and up to 200 in number, rather irregularly arranged and consequently not as 'neat' in appearance as many anemones. The column, visible in closed specimens, has numerous pale suckers, which appear as whitish spots. These spots are not adhesive and, unlike many anemones with suckers on the column, they do not have particles of sand or shell attached to them. The span of tentacles is up to 40mm.

Above: groups of variety *miniata* and *venusta*. St Martins, Isles of Scilly.

Right: a single anemone showing the non-adhesive suckers on the column. Lewis, Hebrides.

There are five recognised colour varieties, which were originally thought to be separate species, and a number of other colour forms.

Variety *miniata* is the most common form. The overall colour is between brown, buff and orange with the disk and tentacles with similar colours and often variegated. The tentacles are usually banded and a common variation has a rayed appearance with light lines from the mouth across the disk and onto the tentacles. This variety is most easily confused with other similar species such as *Sagartia troglodytes* and *Cereus peduncluatus* but both of these are normally found in sand and gravelley areas whereas *S. elegans* is on rock. Both of these other species also have suckers on the column but they are adhesive and normally have fragments of sand and shell attached.

Variety *rosea* has bright pink or rose red tentacles, often with a lighter disk. It is a bright and prominent anemone and unlikely to be confused with anything else.

Variety *nivea* has both the disk and tentacles bright translucent white in colour. It could be confused with white specimens of *Actinothoe sphyrodeta* but *S. elegans* var. *nivea* has many more tentacles, is neater in appearance and has white suckers on the column which *A. sphyrodeta* does not.

Variety *venusta* has a bright plain orange coloured disk with contrasting white tentacles. It could also be confused with the 'fried egg' form of *Actinothoe sphyrodeta*.

Variety *aurantiaca* is the rarest colour variety and may be a south westerly variety – records are from south Wales and Devon. Its' disk is greyish in colour with dull orange tentacles. It is very similar in appearance to the '*decorata*' colour form of *S. troglodytes* though the habitat and presence of adhesive suckers in the latter should distinguish them.

Top: variety *miniata*. St Abbs, Borders.

Centre: variety *nivea*. Summer Isles, Highland.

Bottom: variety *venusta*. St Martins, Isles of Scilly.

Above: a redder form of variety *rosea*. Manacles, Cornwall.

Below: variety *rosea*. Hand Deeps, Devon.

Elegant anemones are found attached to rocks on the shore and down to 50m depth. Shore specimens are found in pools, under stones, in caves or beneath overhangs. They commonly occur in crevices or holes into which they can withdraw if disturbed. Sublittorally they are found on open rock surfaces often in very large numbers packed closely together. They reproduce primarily by basal laceration and thus the large groups are normally all of one colour variety. A typical habitat in south-western England is at the top of vertical rock faces where the topmost metre of the cliff is covered with elegant anemones and the remainder equally densely covered with jewel anemones.

The elegant anemone is both common and widely distributed around all coasts of Britain and Ireland. In Europe it is found north to Scandinavia and Iceland and south into the Mediterranean.

Actinothoe sphyrodeta Fried egg or sandaled anemone

This anemone has plain colours and up to 100 irregularly arranged tentacles which have a stout base and taper to the tips. The size is up to 50mm across the span of the tentacles. The column is smooth, without suckers or other features. It is rather uneven in colour, sometimes with longitudinal patches of pure white on a duller background forming stripes. There are two colour forms to the disk and tentacles. Most commonly both are bright white but some species have an orange disk with white tentacles (the fried egg form).

Above: open and closed anemones showing the lines on the column. Coll, Hebrides.

Left: the 'fried egg' colour form. Salcombe, Devon.

This is another common anemone that grows in rocky areas and is rather similar in appearance to two of the varieties of *Sagartia elegans*. The white form could be confused with *S. elegans* var. *nivea* and the fried egg form with *S. elegans* var. *venusta*. The two distinguishing features are the column, which does not have suckers and often has longitudinal lines and the smaller number of tentacles with a tapering form and less tidy appearance.

Actinothoe sphyrodeta reproduces asexually by longitudinal fission and often occurs in groups. These do not tend to be so closely packed as *S. elegans* nor do they cover large areas. This anemone is almost entirely sublittoral, though it may occasionally occur in overhanging situations on the lower shore. It is normally found on open rocky surfaces but may also attach to other firm surfaces such as kelp holdfasts. It likes water movement and can tolerate turbulent conditions.

This anemone is common on southern and western coasts of Britain and Ireland and occurs as far north as Orkney. It does not have a satisfactory common name as yet. Gosse named it the sandaled anemone after the stripes on the column. The fried egg name is appropriate for the orange and white form but not for the plain white one.

A group of white specimens. Manacles, Cornwall.

SS

Jewel and elegant anemones. St. Kilda.

Sea anemones
Hexacorallia, Order Actinaria

Anemones that live on the shore and in shallow water

The following anemones all normally occur on the lower shore, in rock pools and in shallow water. This is not an exclusive list by any means as many of the other anemones that also occur below low water can be found in the shallows and on the shore.

Actinia equina Beadlet anemone

SSh

The beadlet anemone is one of the most common anemones of the shore and intertidal pools. It is frequently seen as a red jelly-like blob left on rocks that the tide has exposed or as expanded anemones in rock pools. Its colour is usually a deep red but it may also be various shades of brown, orange or green. The anemone is normally a single colour with no differentiation between the column and tentacles. However some specimens may have blue or yellowish spots or streaks on the column. It often has a hump in the centre of the disk which elevates the mouth. The beadlet anemone is up to 50mm across the base and 70mm across the tentacles.

SD

Above: mixed colours of beadlet anemones in a rock pool. Wembury, Devon.

Right: closed anemones exposed at low water. Jersey, Channel Islands.

The beadlet anemone does not reproduce asexually, unlike many anemones. Instead it reproduces viviparously, producing fully formed young individuals which are born through the anemone's mouth.

Whilst this anemone can be found in the shallow sublittoral it is normally encountered between high and low water mark. It can be attached to any firm structure, normally rock, but may also be on wooden or metal piles or concrete breakwaters. It can tolerate reduced salinity and thus also occurs in brackish situations.

Beadlet anemones are very widespread and are common on all coasts of Britain and Ireland. Elsewhere they occur over the whole of Western Europe from Russia in the north to West Africa.

The different forms of the beadlet anemone were for many years thought to be a single species. However two other closely related species are now recognised and it is possible there may be others.

PN

A single, typically red, beadlet anemone. Oban, Argyll and Bute.

Actinia fragacea Strawberry anemone

The strawberry anemone is similar in form to the beadlet but grows to a larger size, 80mm across the base and 100mm across the tentacles. It is always red or dark red in colour and has small flecks or spots of green, yellow or blue over the whole of the column, giving it its' common name. The tentacles are plain red. Unlike the beadlet anemone it is not known to reproduce viviparously.

The strawberry anemone is found in on the lower shore and often in shaded places. Like the beadlet it may be attached to any suitable firm structure.

This anemone is much less common than the beadlet and most records are from the English Channel and south-west England. It has been recorded, however, from all costs of Britain and the west coast of Ireland.

Lizard, Cornwall.

Actinia prasina

Both photos Isle of Man.

This anemone has only been identified as a separate species as recently as 1984 from specimens in the Isle of Man. It is light green in colour and has 100–160 irregularly arranged tentacles, rather than 192 in *A. equina*. The specific name comes from the latin *prasinus* meaning leek-green. It occurs on the shore but, like the strawberry anemone, usually lower down than *A. equina*. It also prefers dark, overhanging, surfaces and is rarely found on open rock. The greenish species shown in the picture from Wembury (page 65) is probably a colour form of *A. equina* and not this species.

Actinia prasina was identified from specimens in the Isle of Man and it has also been found in Morecambe Bay. It is not known if it occurs elsewhere. Anemones in the family *Actinia* show significant genetic differences from different locations as a result of their asexual reproduction. There may therefore be a number of genetically differentiated species, especially from island locations.

Anemonia viridis Snakelocks anemone

A particularly brightly coloured specimen. Ballinskelligs Bay, Cork.

The snakelocks anemone is one of the most common and distinctive anemones of the lower shore and shallow sublittoral. The tentacles are long, irregularly arranged and up to 200 in number. The size is very variable but may be up to 18cm across the tentacles. The tentacles are sometimes plain coloured, from a grey-brown to fairly bright green but many specimens have bright purple tips. Occasionally the anemone is seen with longitudinal purple stripes long the tentacles. All three colours are shown in the photographs.

Like its relative on the shore, the beadlet anemone, the tentacles readily latch on to any invasive object, and the stickiness can be felt with a finger tip. The column is very variable in height, often totally obscured by the tentacles, but when it can be seen it is reddish or dark brown, occasionally with lighter longitudinal streaks.

A plain grey coloured specimen. Lundy, Devon.

The snakelocks anemone commonly reproduces by longitudinal fission and consequently there are often a number of individuals close together. It is found in rock pools on the lower shore and attached to rocks, stones or occasionally seaweeds down to about 20m. It enjoys exposed places and is often seen in areas of strong wave action or strong current. However it can also be found in sheltered areas such as seagrass beds.

The snakelocks anemone is common on all southerly and westerly coasts of Britain and Ireland, but rare in eastern England and Scotland.

Above: sponge spider crab *Inachus phalangium*, commonly found in association with snakelocks anemones. Jersey, Channel Islands.

Right: anemone prawn *Periclimenes sagittifer* amongst the tentacles of a snakelocks anemone. This association has only been observed on the south side of the English Channel but is common in the Channel Islands. Jersey, Channel Islands.

Aulactinia verrucosa Gem anemone

The gem anemone has rather bright tentacles which are white but spotted or banded with grey. There are up to 48 tentacles arranged in multiples of six with a span of 60mm. The disk is patterned and variously coloured including green, red and brown. The column is distinctive since it has longitudinal lines of warts. It is pink or grey and most of the warts are darker. However the six main rows are white. The warts in this species are non adhesive and it never has pieces of sand or shell attached.

The gem anemone reproduces sexually and produces fully formed young.

The gem anemone is found mostly on the shore in pools or in clefts amongst rocks, or attached to rock or stones covered with sand. It is a south-westerly species in the British Isles and most records come from Devon, Cornwall and the Channel Islands. However, it has been recorded from a number of locations on the west coasts of Wales and Scotland and from Holy Island on the Northumbrian coast.

Top: expanded anemone amongst gravel in a rock pool. Wembury Bay, Devon.

Centre: small specimen on a rock. Jersey, Channel Islands.

Bottom: closed anemone showing the distinctive lines of warts on the column. Jersey, Channel Islands.

Anthopleura ballii Red-specked pimplet

There are two colour forms of this anemone: yellow and brown. It has up to 96, relatively long, tentacles arranged in multiples of six. They are somewhat untidily arranged and often curled over at their tips. The span of the tentacles is up to 12cm. The column can be long and trumpet shaped when fully extended. It has longitudinal rows of small, non-adhesive warts. These are pale and each is tipped with a red spot.

The brown variety has the disk and tentacles coloured dull chocolate brown, often with a crimson or purplish lustre and flecked all over with specks of grey and white. The column is dull purplish-brown shading to dull orange or crimson towards the base. The yellow variety has the disk and tentacles coloured a pale translucent straw yellow, sometimes shading to pink or rose red and again irregularly flecked with white. The column is similarly coloured with pale warts. The two colour forms are very different with the brown form quite dull and opaque whilst the yellow form can be translucent and often brightly coloured.

Above: a brown specimen amongst gravel. St Martins, Isles of Scilly.

Right: a greeny-brown specimen showing the non-adhesive warts on the column. St Martins, Isles of Scilly.

Anthopleura ballii can be confused with a number of other anemones. The things to look out for are the non-adhesive warts on the column which are characteristic of this species and the gem anemone. However the latter is smaller and has fewer, patterned, tentacles rather than flecked ones. The disk and tentacles are similar to the trumpet anemone but that has a distinct radiating pattern of light lines on the disk rather than the flecks of this species.

The anemone is found in holes or crevices amongst rocks, particularly in old piddock borings, beneath boulders or buried in sand and mud and attached to a firm object beneath the surface. It is usually on the lower shore and pools but can be found as deep as 25 metres. It also occurs in seagrass beds.

This is a southern species which occurs from Sussex westward to the Isles of Scilly. It is also commonly recorded from the west coast of Ireland. Elsewhere it is found in France and south west Europe and in the Mediterranean.

A yellow tentacled anemone. Helford River, Cornwall.

Above: a greeny brown specimen, Lough Hyne, Cork.

Anthopleura thallia Glaucus pimplet

Above: the disk and tentacles. Below: the column showing the lines with adhesive warts, larger at the top of the column than at the base. Both Loch Maddy, North Uist.

This anemone has vertical rows or warts on the column, those at the top of the column, the parapet, being larger than those lower down. They may join together to from a knobbly ridge. Unlike *Anthopleura ballii*, the warts on this species normally have fragments of shell and gravel attached. The tentacles, of which there are up to 100, are rather stiffly held and irregularly arranged. The disk usually has a pale plain circle around the mouth and then a dark pattern on a variegated background. The tentacles can be olive green or grey and speckled with white or plain white and grey. The column is a dull green, brown or grey, sometimes reddish and the warts may be either lighter or darker than the colour of the column itself. There is usually a darker longitudinal line joining the rows. The anemone has a span of 50mm across the tentacles and the column can also be extended to 50mm.

This anemone is almost always found on exposed rocky shores, from mid-tide level to low water. It will be found in pools, crevices or amongst mussel beds. If there is any gravel present it may well bury itself completely in it. This can make it a difficult anemone to find.

The glaucus pimplet was believed to have a very restricted distribution occurring regularly in the extreme south-west of England (Cornwall and the Isles of Scilly), but only rarely elsewhere in south and west Britain. It has not been recorded from Ireland. However, it does occur on the French Atlantic coast. The pictures represent a new record from the Outer Hebrides.

Diadumene cincta

This is a small delicate anemone with a slender column and a translucent orange colour. Though it may be up to 60mm tall the disk is small, little wider than the column. The tentacles, of which there may be up to 200, are long and fine. The slender column is divided into two parts, a scapus and a capitulum, and when not fully extended may appear lop-sided due to irregular contraction. The colour is usually translucent orange but may have a greenish tinge, especially on the disk.

The anemone frequently reproduces by basal laceration and thus there may be large number of individuals close together. It also means that distribution can be very patchy. Where it occurs it is attached to some hard surface, particularly mussels and other bivalve shells. It occurs on the shore in pools and caves, but not in places which dry out at low water. It is a typical inhabitant of areas with reduced or variable salinity such as estuaries, tidal creeks and harbours. However, it can also be found as deep as 40m.

Diadumene cincta has been recorded from all coasts of the British Isles though most records are from the south coasts of England and Wales.

This anemone can be confused with small species of the plumose anemone, *Metridium senile*, which often occurs in the same habitats and may have an orange coloration. *Diadumene*, however, is more elongate and has many fewer tentacles. *Metridium* rarely contracts but if it does will do so smoothly rather than in the jerky and asymmetrical manner characteristic of *Diadumene*.

Above: Worthing, Sussex.

Left: a group of *Diadumene cincta* amongst sponges. Milford Haven, Pembrokeshire.

Aiptaisiogeton pellucidus

This is a very small anemone, rarely more than 10mm across the base, which may be easily confused with other species, including *Diadumene cincta*, and small *Metridium senile*. It has a smooth column and relatively long slender tentacles, which do not generally retract. It reproduces by basal laceration and as a consequence the base often has a rather ragged outline. It also means there may be a number of individuals of different sizes close together. There are two colour forms. The most common is translucent orange with whitish patches at the base of the tentacles. The other has deep pink tentacles.

This anemone lives attached to rocks in holes and crevices from the lower shore down to about 10m depth. It appears to be rare though it may well be under recorded because of its small size. It is known from a few localities in Dorset and Devon and also further south to Biscay and into the Mediterranean. Because of its rarity we have not been able to find an *in situ* photograph.

Pink specimens in an aquarium.

Haliplanella lineata Orange-striped anemone

RM

Aquarium picture, showing lines on column.

The orange-striped anemone is a small, delicate species with long tentacles. The column is distinctly divided into scapus and capitulum with the lower scapus distinctly coloured with orange, yellow or white stripes over a green or brown background. This contrasts with the upper part of the column, the capitulum, which is a translucent grey-green. The anemone is up to 40mm high, though it is often smaller. The tentacles are long and numerous, up to 100 in number. They are translucent, either colourless or pale grey-green usually irregularly flecked with white or grey. They contrast with the disk, which is darker.

This anemone is usually found in sheltered locations on the shore in pools attached to rocks and shells, frequently amongst mussels. It is tolerant of variations in temperature and salinity and frequently occurs in brackish creeks, lagoons and harbours. In the British Isles it has been recorded from a variety of sites including Chichester Harbour, the Falmouth estuary and as far north as Orkney.

The orange-striped anemone appears to have originated in the western Pacific and has since spread to many other regions. It is thought that its spread is likely to have been the result of being carried on ships bottoms or transplanted oysters or other shellfish. Many of the locations are close to shipping lanes and shellfish cultivation areas. Since the anemone normally reproduces asexually, by longitudinal fission, only a single specimen is required to start a new population.

There is some doubt as to the correct name for this species. It was formerly known as *Diadumene luciae*.

Phellia gausapata Warted corklet

Above: a group of *Phellia* amongst tunicates, sponge and bryozoan turf. St. Kilda.

This anemone has up to 120 tentacles which are irregularly arranged. The disc and tentacles are orange, red, brown, or grey usually variegated colours, and the tentacles are vaguely banded. The width across the tentacles is 30mm. It is one of the Sagartiid anemones and the column is covered with rounded tubercules and a tough horny covering which typically has algae, debris or other animals (including bryozoans and worms) attached to it.

It typically occurs in small groups in extremely exposed shallow rocky situations, often in surge gullies in the kelp zone and usually on vertical surfaces. Recent British and Irish records are all from exposed sites in the north-west of Scotland and Ireland such as Shetland, St Kilda, Rockall, Rathlin and Achill Islands. There is also a recent record from the Isles of Scilly.

Worm anemones Family Edwardsiidae

There are seven British members of this family of anemones all of which have a long worm-like column with a rounded base. Most are small and difficult to see, retract quickly and may be at least party nocturnal.

A group of *Edwardsiella carnea* on rock. Loch Carron, Highland.

Edwardsiella carnea

This is the most widespread and common of the group. It is up to 30mm long and 4mm in diameter. The tentacles are long and slender, up to 32 in number and pinkish in colour whilst the disk has white or yellow markings. The column is divided into a scapus and scapulus. The lower scapus is covered in a thick brown cuticle and the rounded base has adhesive spots which it uses to attach to rocks. The upper scapulus is translucent and similar in colour to the disk.

This species lives in holes and crevices in rocks, often in large aggregations. It has a particular preference for old piddock borings. It occurs from mid-tide level to the shallow water offshore. It is usually found in sheltered spots out of the light. It is easily overlooked since if disturbed it retracts its tentacles rapidly, as it does if out of water.

It is a widespread species and has been recorded from all British coasts, though it is most commonly found in the south and west.

Edwardsia claparedii, E. delapiae, E. timida and Scolanthus callimorphus

These are all burrowing anemones which live in mud sand or gravel and are not attached. When *in situ* only the disc and tentacles can be seen. They live in sheltered locations in shallow water and may occur in large groups. They were often found in beds of the eelgrass, *Zostera marina* but since the decline of this habitat are now more often seen in shallow muddy sand areas.

	Edwardsia claparedii	Edwardisa delapiae	Edwardsia timida	Scolanthus callimorphus
NO. OF TENTACLES	16	16	16–32	16
TENTACLE ARRANGEMENT	8+8	8+8	3 cycles	5+11
TENTACLE SPAN	50mm	45mm	40mm	100mm
TENTACLE COLOUR	transparent with white spots	long, transparent and unspotted – almost invisible	translucent pale orange – may have white tips	translucent – brownish towards tips, spotted or banded with white
DISC COLOUR	mainly white but may have a buff pattern	Translucent – patterned with white & brown	Translucent pale orange with opaque white or pale cream pattern	Patterned cream, buff and dark purplish brown
HABITAT	mud and sand, Zostera beds	sand & gravel, Zostera beds	Sand & gravel	Sand & gravel, Zostera beds
DISTRIBUTION IN BRITISH AND IRISH WATERS	widespread – mostly western coasts	one location only – Valentia Island, Co Kerry	Few current-swept locations without wave action in the Irish Sea esp. Menai Strait	Weymouth, Channel Islands and western Ireland

Above: *Edwardsia claparedii* with white disk (left). Sherkin Island, Cork. With patterned disk (right). Lundy, Devon.

Below: *Edwardsia timida* with translucent tentacles (left). With dense white spots on face of tentacles (right). Both Menai Strait, Gwynedd.

Top: *Scolanthus callimorphus*, showing both speckles and bands on tentacles (left). *Scolanthus callimorphus*, emerging from sediment and showing pattern on disk and column (right). Both Roskeeda, Galway.

Right: *Edwardsia delapiae*. Valentia, Cork.

The Starlet anemone, *Nematostella vectensis* and Ivell's anemone, *Edwardsia ivelli*

These two anemones are both known only from brackish water lagoons in southern England where they occur burrowing in soft mud. Both are very rare, and indeed *E. ivelli* is only known from one location in Sussex where it may now no longer be present.

Both anemones are tiny, about 20mm long and 1.5mm in diameter with a span across the tentacles of 10mm, and where they occur may be in large numbers. *N. vectensis* has been recorded at a density of over 10,000 per square metre. Both species occur in shallow lagoons and ponds, usually in depths of less than 1m. They live in fine sand and mud, often with shingle on top, and in the presence of green algae, especially *Chaetomorpha* spp. and the eelgrass *Zostera marina*.

The starlet sea anemone is known from a number of sites in Norfolk, Suffolk, the Solent and Dorset. Both anemones are highly vulnerable to disturbance whether by pollution, eutrophication, or physical damage by coastal defences or development. As a result they have both been protected species under the Wildlife and Countryside Act since 1988.

Nematosella vectensis. Gilkicker Lagoon, Hampshire.

Sea anemones
Hexacorallia, Order Actinaria

Anemones that live on soft sea-beds (sand, gravel and mud)

The following anemones all normally occur buried in sand, gravel and mud with only their oral disk and tentacles above the surface. There are two types; those that have their column attached at the base to a firm object in the sediment, whether a stone or shell, and the truly burrowing anemones which have a column that relies on its length and shape for stability and is not attached to anything in the sediment.

Aureliania heterocera Imperial anemone

This is very distinctive anemone that is unlikely to be mistaken for any other because of its characteristic very short knobbed tentacles. There are up to 150 tentacles and the anemone is up to 70mm across. The colour is varied, often red, but it may be pink, purplish or yellow. Occasionally it is seen with white tentacles that contrast with the body colour.

The imperial anemone lives amongst rocks or with its column buried in sand, gravel or maerl. Its broad base acts as an anchor in the softer sea-beds. It can retract its disk and tentacles very quickly and completely disappear from view.

Two differently coloured imperial anemones. Left: Jersey, Channel Islands. Inset: Loch Carron, Highland.

This is an uncommon anemone and usually seen singly rather than in groups. It occurs on west and south coasts of Britain and Ireland and appears to be most commonly recorded in Scottish sea lochs.

Multicoloured imperial anemones. Top: Kilkeiran Bay, Galway. Bottom: Loch Carron, Highland.

Anemonactis mazeli

This anemone is distinctive because of the knobbed end to each of its tentacles and is unlikely to be confused with anything else. It has 20 stout tentacles each of which has a constriction near the tip, which produces the rounded end. The tentacles are white or orange and usually have brown or purple flecks along them. The anemone is up to 6cm across the tentacles. The column is up to 12cm long and is normally buried in sand or mud.

This is a rare anemone with few records from the English Channel, The Irish Sea and Ireland, most recently from Strangford Lough. It is always found offshore from 20–650m depth.

Above: specimen from north-west Spain.

Left: juvenile specimen from Strangford Lough, Down which lacks the knobbed end to the tentacles.

Sagartia troglodytes

BP

Above: a typically patterned specimen, Menai Strait, Gwynedd.

Below: a brown and orange specimen, Menai Strait, Gwynedd.

BP

This anemone is very variable in colour and pattern which makes identification more difficult than with some species. It is normally found buried in mud, sand or gravel with its base attached to a buried stone or shell. However it may sometimes be seen on rocks, especially where they have a film of sand or silt over them.

There are two similar anemones which were previously thought to be varieties of *Sagartia troglodytes* but are now recognised as separate species. What was previously referred to as the *decorata* variety is *S. troglodytes* and the other form is now *Sagartia ornata*. *Sagartia troglodytes* grows to 50mm across the base and 10cm tall and may come in a variety of colours from dull white through buff, brown and green and may have either plain or patterned disk and tentacles.

This anemone has up to 200 tentacles arranged in multiples of six. On some individuals the innermost ring of six tentacles is prominent and can be accentuated by a contrasting colour pattern. Where this can be seen it is a reliable identification feature, but it is not found on all specimens. The first ring of six tentacles usually has V-shaped markings at the base. The column has suckers and often has fragments of gravel or shell attached to it.

This anemone is found on the lower shore and shallow waters and may occur in areas with reduced salinity such as harbours and estuaries. It is common around all coasts of Britain but seems to be less so around Ireland.

S. troglodytes proved to be an early, but short lived, coloniser of the HMS Scylla which was sunk in Whitsand Bay, Cornwall in March 2004. Within a few months of the sinking there were large numbers of *S. troglodytes* on the flat surfaces of the decking where there was a thin film of sediment. This specimen is known to be an early coloniser of new substrata but by the late autumn all of the animals had disappeared.

A specimen on the deck of HMS Scylla, Summer 2004.

Sagartia ornata

This species is similar to *S. troglodytes* in form but it is generally smaller, about 1.5m across the base and green or brown in colour. It is most commonly found on stones and mussel shells. Information on distribution is very limited because it was formerly included with *Sagartia troglodytes*.

Sagartia sp.

A very distinctive Sagartid anemone can be found on sand and gravel sea-beds whose identity is uncertain. This has a pattern of six dark areas on the tentacles. However the pattern is often incomplete and the tentacle arrangement is not always consistent. This suggests that it is not *Sagartia troglodytes* since this is only known to reproduce sexually and thus is always evenly arranged, however the habitat is unlikely for *Sagartia elegans*. Further research is required.

Dingle, Kerry.

Cereus pedunculatus Daisy anemone

Above: a cluster of daisy anemones of different sizes. St Martins, Isles of Scilly.

Below: a specimen in coarse sand. Isle of Man.

The daisy anemone is one of the larger sediment dwelling anemones and can be as much as 15cm across the disk. The tentacles are short and very numerous, up to 1,000 in a large specimen. The disk and tentacles are mottled in blue-grey and buff and often have minute white flecks. When partly contracted the disk tends to fold up at the edges. The column is trumpet shaped with a wide base but this is not usually visible in life as the disk lays flat on the sea-bed and the column is buried.

This anemone has some similarities with *Sagartia troglodytes* both in colour and pattern but it is generally larger and the tentacles are shorter leaving a larger oral disk.

The daisy anemone occurs at all depths from pools and gullies on the lower shore to at least 50m. Where it occurs in muddy and sand areas it will be attached to a buried object beneath the surface. In these situations there will often be many anemones in the same area.

It is a widespread species around most of Britain and Ireland, but least common on east coasts of England and Scotland.

Sagartiogeton undatus

PN

This anemone has a long column, up to 12cm, with a wide base, which is attached to a stone or shell beneath the surface. The column is a pale yellow colour and has stripes along its length, which may be partly exposed (see upper photograph). There are up to 200 long tentacles, which are arranged in groups of six and are held elegantly when fully expanded. They have a white line along their length and are almost transparent towards the fine tips.

Sagartiogeton undatus is found buried in mud and sand from the lower shore down to 100m or more. It is widely distributed around south and west coasts of Britain and Ireland as far north as Shetland and is found particularly in sheltered locations.

Above: Plymouth Sound, Devon.

Below: Criccieth, Gwynedd.

RH

Sagartiogeton laceratus

SS

This is a relatively tall anemone with a column up to 60mm tall which flares out at the top to a disk which may be 30cm wide. The anemone is very similar in form to *Sagartiogeton undatus* though it is normally smaller, only growing to a height of 60mm. One distinguishing feature is the colour, the column and disk are orange or buff in colour and there is an intricate pattern of dark makings at the foot of each tentacle. There are up to 200 long tentacles. The anemone is often found in small groups, which is the result of its preferred method of reproduction by basal laceration.

Sagartiogeton laceratus can be distinguished from *Sagartiogeton undatus* by its orange colour, smaller size and less tidy looking tentacles.

This anemone may be found either buried in sand and mud or attached to shells, worm tubes or stones. It is exclusively sublittoral. Most records come from sheltered locations such as sea lochs and harbours in Ireland and western Scotland but it has also been recorded from more exposed areas such as Lundy and the Isles of Scilly.

Above: a closely packed group. Skye.

Below: Loch Goil, Argyll and Bute.

MW

Halcampoides elongatus Night anemone

This is a true burrowing anemone. Its column has a rounded base, which is fixed firmly in the sand or gravel but is not attached to anything in the sediment. The column is at least 10cm long when not buried but extends much longer when *in situ*.

The oral disc is very small and the mouth is on a conical protrusion in the centre. There are twelve tentacles which are long and slim and capable of extension up to a span of 15cm.

This is a distinctive anemone, which is widely distributed throughout the world, often recorded from great depths. It is probably much under recorded because it is primarily nocturnal and is retracted into the sediment during the hours of daylight. British records are from a number of widely distributed sites most of which are islands – the North of Mull, Kilkeiran Bay, Galway, the Isle of Man, Skomer and the Channel Islands. It is exclusively sublittoral, being recorded from depths from 10m or deeper.

Halcampoides in soft sediment. Jersey, Channel Islands.

Halcampoides in gravel.

Halcampoides abyssorum

This species is not included in the Species Directory for the British Isles. It is poorly known and was originally described from deep water in the Norwegian and Barents Seas. It has recently been included in a guide to marine life of Northern Europe and illustrated by a photograph from Southern Norway. The photograph (left) from Scotland is clearly the same species and it has also been photographed on the west coast of Ireland and Lundy in Devon. However the identification must be tentative in the light of how little is known of this species.

Ardvasar, Isle of Skye.

Mesacmaea mitchellii Policeman anemone

Lundy, Devon

This is a burrowing anemone which has a pear-shaped column with a rounded base. There are up to 36 tentacles, which are long and finely pointed at he tips. The first cycle of tentacles are seven in number and always held upwards and together, completely covering the mouth. This is a unique feature and makes the anemone unmistakeable.

The policeman anemone is up to 70mm across the tentacles and the disk and the tentacles are intricately patterned in shades of orange, brown and buff.

Mesacmaea is normally found burrowing in sand and gravel. It is rather a rare anemone, only being recorded from relatively few locations. However where it does occur there may be many individuals in the same area. Recent records include the Llyn Peninsula and Skomer in Wales, Kilkeiran Bay in Ireland and Lundy and the North Devon coast in England.

Peachia cylindrica

This is a burrowing anemone that lives with its column buried in sand and gravel but unattached. The column is elongated with a round base and may be as much as 30cm in length. The oral disc is small with a small lobed projection, called a conchula, arising from one side of the mouth. This is distinctive but difficult to see in live specimens underwater. There are twelve long tentacles with a span of up to 12cm. The tentacles are patterned in cream and grey with beautiful chevron markings. The disc may be the same colour or bright white.

Peachia occurs from low water mark to at least 100m and is most common offshore. It is widely distributed around British and Irish coasts only being rare in the east.

Top: Jersey, Channel Islands.

Right: Lizard, Cornwall.

Halcampa chrysanthellum

This is a small burrowing anemone with an elongated worm like column up to 70mm long and buried in sand or mud. There are 12 short tentacles with a spread of about 10mm, which are patterned with alternate opaque and translucent lines. The disc is usually patterned in similar colours but may be yellow white or buff. There are often two opposite plain tentacles. In Strangford Lough the anemones are all white. *Halcampa* can be distinguished from *Peachia cylindrica* by its smaller size and more stubby tentacles.

A patterned specimen with two opposing cream tentacles. Valentia Island, Cork.

A specimen with cream tentacles Tralee Bay, Kerry.

Halcampa is most frequently found in or around eelgrass beds (*Zostera marina*) and most records are from sheltered localities such as Plymouth Sound and the Solent in England and Strangford Lough, Roaringwater Bay and Valentia Harbour in Ireland. There are records too from Scottish sea lochs and islands and north-east England and south-east Scotland

Sea anemones
Hexacorallia, Order Actinaria, Family Hormathiidae

Anemones that live on other animals

Most of the following anemones normally occur in association with other animals. The relationship differs but none of them use their host for food (i.e. they are not parasitic) and in two cases the relationship is a positive one for both partners (i.e. commensal). They are all in the family Hormathiidae and most have a tough leathery texture to the column, which has a wide base often used to adhere to organic substrates, whether alive or dead.

Calliactis parasitica Parasitic anemone

Large specimen with hermit crab. Helford Estuary, Cornwal.

This rather inappropriately named anemone is almost always found living on the shells of hermit crabs, in Britain the common hermit crab *Pagurus bernhardus*. Often there may be more than one anemone on a single hermit crab shell. The relationship between the two species is a commensal, or sharing one. The anemone benefits from the mobility of the hermit crab and access to food. The crab benefits from the protection from predators afforded by the stinging nematocysts of the anemone. This species normally attaches itself to suitable shells without assistance from the crab but elsewhere other hermit crabs actively seek out anemones and place them on their shells. Sometimes the anemones can also be seen on the claws of spider crabs or on bivalve shells as in the photograph on the next page.

Above: small specimen on slipper limpet and scallop shell. Lyme Bay, Devon.

Left: Jersey, Channel Islands.

The anemone has a long column, up to 10cm, and numerous fine tentacles which are not strongly coloured or patterned. They may be up to 700 in number. The column is a dull yellowish in colour with brown and reddish patches and spots, usually forming vertical stripes. This anemone is unlikely to be mistaken for anything else because of its relationship with hermit crabs.

The parasitic anemone is relatively common on the south coast of England and in the Channel Islands. Elsewhere there are also recent records from the north coast of Cornwall and one location in south-west Ireland. There is also a record from the north of Skye.

Adamsia carciniopados Cloak anemone

PN

Hermit crab showing tentacles of the Cloak anemone under the body. Oban, Argyll and Bute.

The cloak anemone lives in association with hermit crabs, in this case *Pagurus prideaux*. The anemone has a very wide base, which is modified to wrap around the hermit crab's shell. The disk and tentacles are underneath the shell and crab and the base covers the shell, meeting over the upper part. In life therefore this is one anemone where it is the base and column which needs to be recognised as the disk and tentacles may be hidden underneath. The tentacles are very close to the mouth of the hermit crab, an ideal location for gathering scraps. The colour of the column is distinctive being white with chestnut shades and almost always covered with pink spots. The tentacles are relatively short and white in colour.

The relationship between the two species is apparently obligatory and neither is seen without the other. This is a contrast with the parasitic anemone where, though it is almost always seen on a hermit crab shell, *Pagurus bernhardus* often occurs without the anemone. The presence of the cloak anemone means that *Pagurus prideaux* does not have to change shells as it grows, a dangerous process. The cloak anemone produces a membrane which effectively increases the capacity of the shell as the crab grows. Its stinging tentacles also offer protection from predators. The anemone also readily emits nematocyst-bearing acontia as an additional protective mechanism.

The cloak anemone is widely distributed around all coasts of Britain and Ireland though it is rare on the east coast of England.

A number of different scientific names have been used for this species and it may be seen named as *Adamsia maculata* or *Adamsia palliata*.

Above left: threatened crab with anemone emitting acontia. Jersey, Channel Islands.
Below: purple spots on the column of *Adamsia*. Oban, Argyll and Bute.

Amphianthus dohrnii Sea fan anemone

Multiple anemones on a pink sea fan. Hilsea Point, Devon

The sea fan anemone lives almost exclusively on the two species of British sea fan though it has been known to occur on other rod-like living structures such as hydroid stems. There is no benefit to the host animal from this association but presumably the anemone benefits from being elevated above the seabed into food-bearing currents.

This is a small anemone, which rarely exceeds 10mm across the disk. The base is modified to wrap around the stem of the host and the whole body may be elongated along the same axis as the stem it is attached to. The tentacles are relatively short and may be up to 80 in number. The colour is buff to pale orange and the tentacles are translucent white. The sea fan anemone normally reproduces by basal laceration which often results in a number of individuals being found on a single host.

The anemone was understood to be quite common in the western English Channel and southern Ireland in the 1920s and 1930s but is now rare. The species also occurs in south-western Europe and in the Mediterranean and appears to be declining throughout its range. There are related species which have a similar lifestyle in tropical waters.

Recent British records come from a number of sites near Plymouth and at the Manacles on the Lizard Peninsula, but even here less than 1% of the pink sea fans, *Eunicella verrucosa*, have anemones present. They have also been seen on the northern sea fan, *Swiftia pallida*, in the Firth of Lorn in western Scotland.

Because of the rarity of this species and its apparent decline it is one for which there is a Biodiversity Species Action Plan. This concentrates largely on increasing information about the species. Action taken to protect the pink sea fan or northern sea fan would also benefit the sea fan anemone.

RH

A single specimen. Firth of Lorn, Argyll and Bute.

RH

Multiple anemones on northern sea fan. Firth of Lorn, Argyll and Bute.

Hormathia coronata

Single specimen amongst stones. Isle of Man.

This anemone is normally found attached to shells or worm tubes but may also be attached to stones, rocks or objects buried in sand. It only occurs sublittorally where it may be found down to 100m. It has a broad base, which is up to 40mm across and may be up to 50mm high. The column has small solid tubercules. The tentacles are moderately long and arranged in multiples of six. The disk and tentacles are reddish or buff, usually with a delicate dark and light pattern. Reproduction is thought to be by viviparity.

It is a westerly species and most recent records come from the west coast of Scotland from Mull northwards to Shetland, and from most coasts of Ireland, except the east. It also occurs in north Wales, south-western England, northern France and elsewhere in south-west Europe.

Two anemones, the right hand one closed up and visible only as a domed lump. Isles of Scilly.

Cataphellia brodricii

Above: two anemones amongst gravel. Aran Islands, Galway.
Below: Isles of Scilly.

This anemone has a wide base, up to 60mm across, which often exceeds the span of the tentacles and a column covered with small solid tubercules. The disc and tentacles have a delicate pattern in yellow, cream and brown. The tentacles are relatively short, arranged in five cycles and up to 96 in number.

Unlike the other hormathids it is not normally found living on living on other animals, though it may occur amongst kelp holdfasts. It is usually encountered on the lower shore and shallow sublittoral in the kelp zone. Here is may be attached to stones, beneath boulders or on rocks with a thin sand covering and often in areas with a moderate current. It is very sensitive to disturbance and retracts quickly making it difficult to find.

Cataphellia is a southerly species which has only been recorded in England from the south coasts of Devon and Cornwall, where it may be found particularly in estuaries such as the Exe, Fowey and Fal. It also occurs in more exposed locations in the Isles of Scilly and southern Ireland, particularly around the Saltee islands and at Sherkin. The picture from the Aran Islands is probably the most northerly record.

Other rare hormathid anemones

There are four other rarely encountered hormathid anemones:

Hormathia digitata is a northerly species was previously frequent on the north-east coast of England but there are no recent records. It normally attaches to whelk and other gastropod shells, either alive or dead. A picture is shown from Norway to encourage recording in our area. For further information and pictures see Moen and Svensen 2004.

Hormathia digitata. Norway.

Hormathia alba is a deep water anemone which has been recorded off south-west Ireland.

Paraphellia expansa lives buried in sand and gravel and has a very wide base which is unattached and acts as an anchor. The column is often encrusted with sand. It is thought to occur in the English Channel, the Irish Sea and south-west Ireland but the only recent record is from Barra in the Outer Hebrides.

Actinauge richardii is an unusual anemone in that it does not usually live attached to a hard surface, nor does it burrow deep into soft sediments. Instead its base is able to form an almost enclosed cup within which it encloses a ball of mud or sand. This allows it to live unattached with the ball acting as a sea anchor. It is a deep water anemone, always found offshore in depths of over 50m. It has a wide distribution but is not likely to be seen by divers.

Jewel anemone wall. The Manacles, Cornwall.

Corallimorpharians
Hexacorallia, Order Corallimorpharia

Corallimorpharians are effectively corals without a skeleton. Their internal anatomy, nematocysts and tentacles are identical to the hard corals. There are many tropical species but only one occurs in British and Irish waters.

Corynactis viridis Jewel anemone

The jewel anemone is one of the most dramatic and often photographed of all the British and Irish sea anemones. It can be easily distinguished from almost all other anemones by the knobbed end to each of its tentacles. Although each anemone is a separate individual they reproduce by longitudinal fission in which an individual first stretches itself and then splits across the middle creating two new anemones of equal size. This leads to large groups of densely packed cloned individuals on rock faces, often covering several square metres. The individual anemones are up to 10mm across but have relatively long columns up to twice the width. When the tentacles are retracted they look like little coloured warts on the rock face.

Mixed group. Isles of Scilly.

Jewel anemones are brightly coloured, ranging from pink (which looks blue underwater), through purple and bright emerald green to orange and brown, often with contrasting colours to the knobbed tips of the tentacles. These are colour varieties and not different species. Normally the colour varieties are found in groups rather than mixed, due to the reproductive process.

Jewel anemones have been recorded from the lower shore and shallow waters where they are found in caves and under overhangs. However they are most common sublittorally, on vertical and overhanging rock faces as deep as 80m.

The jewel anemone is found in rocky areas along the south and west coasts of England, Wales, Scotland and Ireland. It is particularly common on clear offshore reefs. Generally the anemones towards the southern extent of the range appear to be bigger than those in the north and they grow larger in conditions where there is a strong surge and clear water.

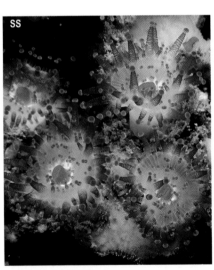

Above: Aran Islands, Galway.

Right: examples of different coloured jewel anemones from Devon and Donegal.

Hard Corals
Hexacorallia Order Scleractinia

As their name suggests these corals have a hard external skeleton and are also known as stony corals. Their tough exterior, known as a **corallum**, is secreted from the walls and base of the anemone-like polyp and is made almost completely of calcium carbonate. In times of danger or when not feeding the **polyp** can completely withdraw inside the hard outer cup and, also like an anemone, its tentacles contain stinging cells. The top and inside of the corallum comprises of a series of vertical radial plates or **septa** which correspond to the mesenteries of the polyp itself.

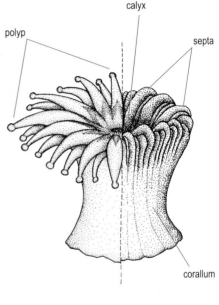

Some species of hard coral are solitary, living as separate individuals, although there may be many others of the same species nearby. Others consist of many corallites fused together to form a colony. All are slow growing and fragile. Hard corals reproduce by releasing eggs and sperm which combine in the water column to form free-swimming larvae. The colonial corals are also able to reproduce asexually by budding new polyps. Colonial corals are the reef-building corals of the tropics and there are a large number of species worldwide.

There are 12 species of hard corals in British waters of which only one, the Devonshire cup-coral, is common. We have included seven of the species in this book. Two of the others (*Balanophyllia celluosa* and *Leptopsammia britannica*) are deep water species and the other three (*Flabellum macandrewi*, *Stenocyathus vermiformis* and *Dendrophyllia cornigera*) are not included in recent literature.

Of the species included, five are solitary corals and only two colonial corals. One of these is very small and does not contribute to reef formation. The other, *Lopelia pertusa*, is a cold water coral which, together with other corals, forms substantial reefs in very deep waters.

Caryophyllia smithii Devonshire cup-coral

Above: a white polyp completely covering the corallum. Firth of Lorn, Agyll and Bute.
Below: two coloured variety from Loch a Chairn Bhain, Highland.

Of all the hard corals this is the most common and widespread. Despite its name this solitary coral is found not just in Devon but around most of the British and Irish coasts apart from the south east and much of the east coast of England and Scotland. It grows up to 3cm across and occurs in a variety of jewel-like colours, often with a zigzag of contrasting colour around the centre, and a white knob on the end of each transparent tentacle. When fully expanded this coral is easily mistaken for an anemone but when the tentacles are withdrawn the white calcareous 'cup' is obvious. It grows attached to rocks and on shipwrecks from the low water mark down to at least 100m. In some cases there are one or several tiny barnacles, *Boscia anglica*, growing on the side of the cup and distorting its shape.

Two coloured varieties from Lundy, Devon.

Two corallites with the polyps retracted and with a number of barnacles on the sides. Lundy, Devon.

A small cluster. Jersey, Channel Islands.

This small coral forms solitary cups less than 1cm across. It is much smaller than the Devonshire cup-coral and is circular rather elliptical in shape. It has knobbed, transparent or plain coloured tentacles. It lives in shaded cracks and crevices and has only been reported from a few locations around the British Isles including sites in Wales, western Scotland, south-west Ireland, Devon, Dorset and the Channel Islands. It may be more widespread but is easily overlooked. It is a solitary coral but often found in small compact groups of individuals.

Right: part of a group of corals. Worbarrow, Dorset.

Balanophyllia regia Scarlet-and-gold cup-coral

This is a small cup-coral which does not exceed 2.5cm in diameter. It has a deep yellow or orange centre and up to 48 translucent tentacles covered in tiny yellow warts which contain the stinging cells. The tentacles do not have knobs on the end. It is confined to the extreme south and west of the British Isles as far north as The St David's Peninsula in Pembrokeshire. It grows in crevices, gullies and on rock faces from the low water mark down to around 25m. Most records are from shallow water, often just below the low tide mark and in areas where there may be considerable surge.

Again, although this is a solitary cup-coral, where it does occur, there are often a number of individuals close together.

The only other bright yellow cup-coral is the sunset cup-coral, which is bigger and lacks the darker coloured disk.

Skomer, Pembrokeshire

Leptopsammia pruvoti Sunset cup-coral

The largest and most striking of all the cup-corals is also one of the rarest. The sunset cup-coral grows to 5cm across and is an intense golden yellow or orange colour. There are 96 tentacles, each with a more intensely coloured knob on the end.

A cluster of sunset cup-corals. Sark, Channel Islands.

The sunset cup-coral is known only from a few sites in the Isles of Scilly, Lundy, south Devon, Lyme Bay and the Channel Islands and grows on shaded rock faces, gullies or overhangs. It lives well below the low water line down to around 40m and, though it is a solitary coral, it is often found in groups of between ten and several hundred individuals. Long term studies have shown that this slow-growing coral can live to be over 100 years old but reproduces very infrequently making it vulnerable to disturbance. This, and its rarity, have caused it to be listed in the UK Biodiversity Action Plan. There is evidence from monitoring that the numbers of corals at Lundy is decreasing with losses exceeding new recruits.

Above: a single coral. Sark, Channel Islands.

Like other cup-corals, the barnacle *Boscia anglica* is commonly found attached to the corallum, as in the picture from Lyme Bay. Two worms, the horseshoe worm *Phoronis hippocrepia* and a fan worm *Potamilla reniformis* are also known to bore into the base of the corallum and can cause detachment from the rocky surface and hence lead to the death of the coral.

Below: closed corals heavily infested with barnacles (the small white corals are *Caryophyllia inornata*). Lyme Bay, Dorset.

Sphenotrochus andrewianus Wedge coral

This is the smallest of all the cup-corals and as such is easily overlooked. It grows unattached in coarse sand or shingle and has a wedge shaped cup that only reaches 12mm in length when fully grown. Little is known about the colour of this coral's polyp but it is thought to have up to 24 knobbed tentacles. The juvenile of this species sometimes has a crown of tentacles at both ends of the cup. The wedge coral has been recorded in the past around all of the British Isles but was not seen in any of the major recent diver surveys around Britain and Ireland. It lives from around 9m down to at least 100m.

Hoplangia durotrix Weymouth carpet coral

Above: Jersey, Channel Islands. Below: Purbeck, Dorset.

This rare colonial coral forms clusters up to 5cm across. It grows well hidden in caves and crevices out of the light from low water down to around 25m. It is thought to only feed at night. It was given its common name after first being found near Weymouth but recent records are also from the Channel Islands, South Devon, the Isles of Scilly and Skomer.

Its appearance is very similar to *Caryophyllia inornata* but the clusters are much more closely fused together with a common base, though this is not always visible.

Lophelia pertusa Deepwater coral

This is by far the largest of all the corals, hard or otherwise, growing in the seas around the British Isles but as it lives in water between 50–3,000m it is rarely seen.

Lophelia grows in colonies which can vary enormously in size. Most British records are of colonies up to 10m in diameter which could be hundreds of years old. However a reef surveyed on the Sula Ridge off Norway in 250m of water was found to be more than 13 kilometers in length and up to 30m high. *Lophelia* lacks zooxanthellae and thus relies entirely on filtering food from the sea water. Consequently it lives in areas with strong water currents. Because of the large size of the *Lophelia* reefs it has been described as the 'rainforest of the sea' as it provides a rich habitat for many other species of marine life. There are other species of deep water corals but *Lophelia* is the only one which might occur within diving depths.

ES

Most British records come from the edge of the Scottish continental shelf, off the Outer Hebrides and west of the Shetlands as well as around Rockall and to the west of Ireland. However a new *Lophelia* reef was discovered in 2004 in the southern part of The Minch between the Scottish mainland and the Outer Hebrides. This is the first significant reef discovered in British inshore waters. Elsewhere in the North-east Atlantic locations include the narrow areas of some Norwegian fijords (from where the photograph comes). *Lophelia* also occurs in deep waters in the Mediteranean Sea, along the coasts of eastern North America, Brazil, West Africa and on the mid-Atlantic Ridge. *Lophelia* has also been known to colonise artifical structures such as the legs of oil rigs.

Athough they only occur in deep waters, *Lophelia* reefs are increasingly threatened by deep water fishing and oil exploration. Because so little is known of their growth rates and biology they are another species for which the UK has prepared a Biodiversity Action Plan.

In 2003 an emergency ban on bottom trawling in the area of the Darwin Mounds north of the Outer Hebrides was introduced to protect the *Lophelia* reefs. The ban became permanent in August 2004 and covers an area of 100 square kilometers. The site is also a proposed Special Area of Conservation (cSAC) under the Habitats Directive.

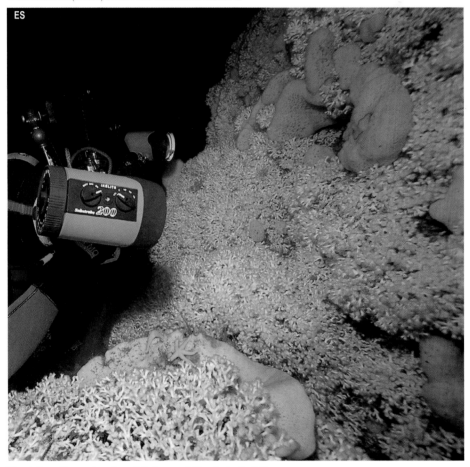

The shallowest known *Lopelia* reefs in Europe - in Trondheimsfjord, Norway.

Conservation of sea anemones and corals in Britain and Ireland

Much publicity has been given to human and climate change impacts on tropical coral reefs, many of which are in serious decline. There are also conservation issues for temperate water corals and anemones.

Cold water reef-building corals

The only reef-building corals in British and Irish seas are in very deep water on the edge of the continental shelf. Here the *Lophelia* reefs were for many years too deep to be affected by human activities. However overfishing of shallow water fish stocks and the use of larger fishing vessels have led to an expansion of deep water fisheries and in particular bottom trawling. This has the potential of destroying extensive areas of deep water reef over a short period.

Publicity of the threat to deep water reefs has led to the identification of a 100km² area known as the Darwin Mounds north east of Rockall and west of Fair Isle as a UK Special Area of Conservation under the EU Habitats Directive. Bottom trawling was banned under emergency measures in 2003 and a permanent ban came into force in August 2004. This ban, however, only covers a small area of reef and the overall problem is more widespread. Ireland has recently proposed SACs for the protection of *Lophelia* in Irish waters and has asked the EU for a ban of fishing in these areas.

A second concern about the future of *Lophelia* reefs comes from the exploitation of oil and gas fields on the edge of the continental shelf. The difficulties of access and our limited knowledge of the extent and status of deep water reefs are all barriers to effective conservation.

Biodiversity Action Plans

As a part of its response to the Rio Earth Summit the UK government has established an action planning process aimed at maintaining habitat and species diversity. The resulting biodiversity action plans (BAPs) operate both at a national and local level and involve not only the official conservation bodies but also non-governmental organisations such as the Marine Conservation Society and the Wildlife Trusts. Seasearch studies are contributing to our knowledge and conservation of a number of the BAP species.

Whilst there are relatively few marine species on the BAP species list, anemones and corals are prominently represented. The species are:

pink sea fan	*Eunicella verrucosa*
tall sea pen	*Funiculina quadrangularis*
sea fan anemone	*Amphianthus dohrnii*
starlet anemone	*Nematostella vectensis*
Ivell's anemone	*Edwardsia ivelli*
sunset cup-coral	*Leptopsammia pruvoti*
deepwater coral	*Lophelia pertusa*

These anemones and corals fall into three groups:

The pink sea fan, the sea fan anemone (which lives on it) and the sunset cup-coral are all characteristic species of south-westerly rocky reefs. The pink sea fan and sunset cup-coral are both long-lived species whose presence on a reef demonstrates stability in the conditions they need to survive over a number of decades. On the other hand little is known about the biology of the sea fan anemone, though populations are believed to have declined significantly since the 1950s. Studies carried out through Seasearch are at an early stage but suggest that the anemones are either short-lived or very mobile as their presence on individual sea fans varies.

The sea fan anemone and sunset cup-coral are both categorised as nationally rare species whilst the pink sea fan is nationally scarce. Sea fans were collected in the 1960 and 70s as souvenirs and it is consequently one of very few marine species protected from intentional damage or disturbance by the Wildlife and Countryside Act.

Collection as souvenirs has ceased but the species faces a much bigger threat from bottom trawling and entanglement in monofilament fishing nets. This has led to a voluntary ban on scallop dredging in parts of Lyme Bay where the extent of damage to sea fan populations was shown to be extremely high. Nevertheless, after winter storms large numbers of sea fans are regularly washed up tangled in netting on Chesil Bank at the eastern end of Lyme Bay.

Chesil Beach, Dorset.

Seasearch studies have shown that the highest incidence of sea fan anemones is on sea fans at the Manacles on the Lizard peninsula in Cornwall. This site has no special conservation status.

It is perhaps surprising that the northern sea fan, *Swiftia pallida*, is not identified as a BAP species since it has a narrower range of distribution than the pink sea fan, at least in inshore waters. It is also host to the sea fan anemone.

The starlet anemone and Ivell's anemone are both brackish water, lagoonal, species. They are therefore extremely vulnerable to loss of habitat from development activities or localised pollution effects. It is quite possible that Ivell's sea anemone has become extinct as it was only known from a single lagoon in West Sussex where it has not been found for some years. Most of the sites where the starlet anemone occurs are designated as Sites of Special Scientific Interest. However one of the actions in the BAP for this species is to increase the number of sites where they are found by habitat creation.

The tall sea pen is found in a number of Scottish sea lochs and is thought to have been badly affected by trawling for scampi which live in the same habitat.

Marine Protected Areas (MPAs)

1. Marine Nature Reserves

The legal basis in the UK for the establishment of Marine Nature Reserves (MNRs) is the Wildlife and Countryside Act 1981. In over 20 years since the legislation was passed only three MNRs have been established, Lundy in Devon, Skomer in south Wales and Strangford Lough in Northern Ireland.

Of the anemone and coral BAP species pink sea fans are found in two of the three MNRs, Lundy and Skomer, and sunset cup-corals are also found at Lundy. Sadly, work carried out by the Marine Conservation Society and Seasearch has shown that populations of both species are in decline at Lundy.

The MNR legislation does not allow fishing activity to be controlled in Marine Nature Reserves. That would have to be done by Sea Fisheries Committee Bylaws and it was not until 2004 that part of Lundy was made a statutory no take zone. However it is unlikely that the level of fishing at either Lundy or Skomer is having any adverse effect on the sea fans and cup-corals.

Active monitoring takes place at Skomer which includes the sea fan populations. There has been much less monitoring around Lundy and the concerns about the state of sea fans, cup-corals and other life have been expressed by the Marine Conservation Society, Seasearch and the Marine Biological Association. A monitoring survey was carried out by consultants for English Nature in 2004 but the conclusions were not available at the time of writing.

In Ireland Nature Reserves are designated under the Wildlife Act of 1976 and currently there are three reserves with a large marine component. Lough Hyne in Co. Cork was designated in 1981 and was the first marine nature reserve in Britain and Ireland. The other two reserves are Inch Strand in Co. Kerry and the Bull Island in Co. Dublin.

Right: a sea fan suffering from die back from the base with only the tops of the branches alive. Manacles, Cornwall.

2. Special Areas of Conservation

English Nature, Countryside Council for Wales, Scottish Natural Heritage, the Environment and Heritage Service in Northern Ireland and the National Parks and Wildlife Service in Ireland have identified Special Areas of Conservation (SACs) arising out of the requirements of the EU Habitats Directive. There is a requirement to monitor biodiversity in these areas and to act to protect them.

In the UK a number of the SACs cover reef areas and include sites where the pink sea fan, sea fan anemone and sunset cup-coral all occur, such as the Isles of Scilly and Lundy. However there are a number of important sites where there is no special protection and, as a result of studies, the Marine Conservation Society and Seasearch have recommended changes and additions to SACs to protect all three species in South Wales, the Manacles, Plymouth and Dorset.

Ireland has a number of SACs for reefs in which the sea fan occurs. The Valentia Harbour/Portmagee channel SAC has the very rare anemone *Edwardsia delapiae*. This anemone has not been found anywhere else and is Ireland's only known marine endemic species.

Other conservation measures

Sites of Special Scientific Interest (SSSIs) are commonly used on land to protect important habitats and species. However they cannot extend below low water mark and are therefore not generally appropriate for marine sites. However enclosed lagoons and intertidal areas can be included and many of the locations where starlet sea anemone occurs are SSSIs. There is no equivalent legislation at present to protect areas below the low water mark..

Three of the British anemones and corals are also protected species under the Wildlife and Countryside Act. The two lagoonal species, the starlet anemone and Ivell's anemone, became protected in 1988 and the pink sea fan, in 1992. This means that it is offence to kill, injure, take, possess or offer these animals for sale.

In Ireland Natural Heritage Areas (NHAs) can be designated under the Wildlife amendment Act 2000 and a number of marine areas were proposed as NHAs. To date none have been formally designated.

Seasearch

Seasearch is a volunteer underwater survey project for recreational divers to record observations of marine habitats and the life they support. The information gathered is used to increase our knowledge of the marine environment and contribute towards its conservation.

Seasearch data has helped to define the boundaries of areas for conservation, recorded the presence of rare and unusual species and provided information for local groups to campaign for protection of their local marine life and habitats. The data is held both by local record centres and centrally and is available for anyone to consult on the internet through the National Biodiversity Network (NBN). Go to **www.searchnbn.net** to see it.

Divers can participate in Seasearch training courses at different levels suitable to their knowledge and experience. These include the Observer Course which gives an introduction to marine habitat and species identification and survey methods. The Surveyor Course is for more experienced recorders and there are also Specialist Courses which provide participants with more information on specific groups of marine life or additional survey techniques.

In addition to a national coordinator for the project, there is also a network of local coordinators in many coastal areas who organise Seasearch survey dives and training. We can also provide training and talks in other areas on demand. For further information see the Seasearch website at www.seasearch.org.uk

Seasearch is co-ordinated for the UK by a Steering Group led by the Marine Conservation Society and including representatives from statutory conservation bodies (Countryside Council for Wales, English Nature, Scottish Natural Heritage, the Environment and Heritage Service, Northern Ireland and the Joint Nature Conservation Committee), the Environment Agency, the Wildlife Trusts, the Marine Biological Association (MarLIN), diver training organisations (BSAC, PADI, SAA and SSAC), Nautical Archaeological Society and independent marine life experts. Seasearch is financially supported by the Heritage Lottery Fund and the statutory conservation bodies.

www.seasearch.org.uk

About the author

Chris Wood has been diving in the waters around the British Isles for over thirty years and is passionate about the marine life he has encountered. A self-taught marine naturalist and underwater photographer, he has taken part in marine survey projects all over the world. An active supporter of the Marine Conservation Society, Chris oversees their popular series of trips for diving members and is the National Coordinator for Seasearch, an underwater survey programme for volunteer divers. Both of these projects, along with his vibrant photographs and presentations, have introduced thousands of divers and non-divers to the fascinating world of British and Irish marine life.

The author recording pink sea fans in the Isles of Scilly.

Photo left: elegant anemone *Sargatia elegans*.

Books and Websites

Books

British Anthozoa by R. L. Manuel (1981) Linnean Society, London.
The most recent complete review of British Anthozoa and the source of much of the information in this book. Also contains detailed information on each species and is illustrated by beautiful line drawings. There is an extensive bibliography.

The Anthozoa of the British Isles – a colour guide by R. L. Manuel (1980) Underwater Conservation Society
Long unavailable this 'miniprint guide' was the first attempt to provide information and colour pictures of British Anthozoa to help the marine naturalist. It has been an important source of information and I hope this book will be as useful to readers in the future as my dog eared copy of the guide has been to me in the past.

Actinologica Britannica: **A History of the British Sea-anemones and corals by P. H. Gosse (1860)** Van Voorst, London
The first review of the British Sea anemones and corals and the source of many of the original descriptions of the species. Whilst many of the names have subsequently changed and a number of species have been combined or separated, it is astonishing how much had been described 150 years ago, long before the advent of the diving surveys that have allowed us to see many of these species in their natural habitats.

The Species Directory of the Marine Fauna and Flora of the British Isles and Surrounding Seas. Eds. Christine M. Howson and Bernard E. Picton (1997) Ulster Museum and Marine Conservation Society
The species checklist for all British marine fauna and flora. A valuable resource for names, spellings, synonyms and literature sources.

There are a number of general field guides which contain a selection of the sea anemones and corals found in this book. They are a useful source of additional photographs as so often looking at more than one image can help with identification. I list a small selection of recent guides that I have found useful.

Sussex Marine Life – an identification guide for divers by Robert Irving (1998) Sussex Seasearch

Marine Life of the Channel Islands by Sue Daly (1998) Kingdom Books, Waterlooville

Great British Marine Animals by Paul Naylor (2003) Sound Diving Publications

Marine Fish and Invertebrates of Northern Europe by Frank Emil Moen and Erling Svensen (2004) Kom, Norway and Aquapress, Southend on Sea

Websites

Encyclopedia of Marine Life of Britain and Ireland

www.habitas.org.uk/marinelife/index.html

Based in the Ulster Museum and maintained by Bernard Picton and Christine Morrow, this photographic guide covers a selection of the larger animals which live round the coasts of Britain and Ireland. It is intended for divers and marine biologists who need to be able to recognise species *in situ* and is illustrated by underwater pictures. It is a good source for updated information on species and contains other images of almost all of the anemones and corals included in this book.

MarLIN The Marine Life Information Network for Britain and Ireland

www.marlin.ac.uk/

Based at the Marine Biological Association in Plymouth the site contains Biology and Sensitivity Reviews for Key Species, These provide much information about the selected species including many of the species in this book. There are photographs of all of the species included.

Joint Nature Conservation Committee

www.jncc.gov.uk/

The Marine section of the site contains information on protected sites, habitats and species and includes the Marine Habitat Classification for the UK which is used in professional level surveys.

Joint Nature Conservation Committee – Mermaid

www.jncc.gov.uk/mermaid/

This is the site where all the Marine Nature Conservation Review and other data – including Seasearch data up to about 2000 can be searched and viewed. Good for seeing where anemones have been recorded in the past and what else was there. Will eventually migrate to the NBNGateway but a useful source of information for now.

National Biodiversity Network – NBN Gateway

www.searchnbn.net/

This site allows you to view distribution maps and download UK wildlife data by using a variety of interactive tools. It is completely dependent on the data providers and coverage is patchy. This is to be the public repository for all Seasearch information and has the benefit that you can search for marine data from a number of sources on a single search.

UK Biodiversity Action Plan

www.ukbap.org.uk

This site includes all of the Species and Habitat Action Plans and is the source of information for everything about the Biodiversity Action Planning process.

Seasearch

www.seasearch.org.uk

The site for all the information about Seasearch and how to take part. You can download recording forms and guidance and find out what courses and diving surveys are planned in your area.

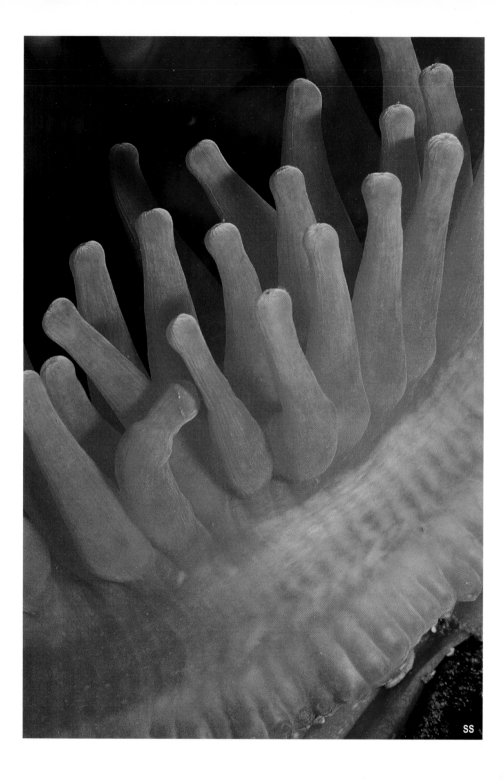

SS

Index

snakelocks anemone 9, 18, **68**, **69**
soft corals 7, 10, 11, 15, 19
southern cup-coral 18, **108**
Special Area of Conservation 114, 118
Sphenotrochus andrewianus 112
spirocysts 10
sponge spider crab *69*
starlet anemone 17, **80**, 115, 116, 118
Stenocyathus vermiformis 105
stolon 9
Stolonifera 7, 15, 35
Stoloniferans 7, 15, 35
Stomphia coccinea 16, **53**
Strangford Lough 117
strawberry anemone 16, **66**
sunset cup-coral 18, **110, 111,** 115, 116, 117
Swiftia pallida 15, *25*, **29**, 98, 116
swimming anemone 16, **53**

─────── **T** ───────

tall sea pen 15, **32**, 115
tentacles 8
transverse fission 12, 55
Tritonia hombergi 20, *21*
Tritonia nilsodhneri 27
trumpet anemone 16, **55**, **56**
trumplet anemone 55
tube anemones 7, 9, 11, 15, 37

─────── **U** ───────

UK Special Area of Conservation 115
Urticina eques 16, **51**, **52**, 53
Urticina felina 16, **49**, **50**

─────── **V** ───────

verrucae 8
Virgularia mirabilis 15, **33**, *81*
viviparity 11, 55
viviparously 66

─────── **W** ───────

warted corklet 17, **77**
wedge coral 12, 18, **112**
Weymouth carpet coral 18, **112**
white cluster anemone 16, **45**
Wildlife and Countryside Act 14, 28, 80, 116, 118
worm anemones 17, **78**, **79**, **80**

─────── **Y** ───────

yellow cluster anemone 16, *41*, *44*, **43**

─────── **Z** ───────

Zoantharia 7, 16, 41
zoantharians 41
zooplankton 25
zooxanthellae 113
Zostera marina 78, 80, 92